A Walk in the Night
with Zhuangzi

SUNY Series in Chinese Philosophy and Culture

Roger T. Ames, editor

A Walk in the Night with Zhuangzi

Musings on an Ancient Chinese Manuscript

KUAN-YUN HUANG

Cover image: "Bamboo and Poem" / Zhu Lu (Chinese, 1553–1632) / early 17th century. The Metropolitan Museum of Art.

Published by State University of New York Press, Albany

© 2023 State University of New York

All rights reserved

Printed in the United States of America

No part of this book may be used or reproduced in any manner whatsoever without written permission. No part of this book may be stored in a retrieval system or transmitted in any form or by any means including electronic, electrostatic, magnetic tape, mechanical, photocopying, recording, or otherwise without the prior permission in writing of the publisher.

For information, contact State University of New York Press, Albany, NY
www.sunypress.edu

Library of Congress Cataloging-in-Publication Data

Name: Huang, Kuan-yun, 1978– author.
Title: A walk in the night with Zhuangzi : musings on an ancient Chinese manuscript / Kuan-yun Huang.
Other titles: Fan wu liu xing.
Description: Albany : State University of New York Press, [2023] | Series: SUNY series in Chinese philosophy and culture | Includes bibliographical references and index.
Identifiers: LCCN 2022022713 | ISBN 9781438491776 (hardcover : alk. paper) | ISBN 9781438491783 (ebook) | ISBN 9781438491769 (pbk. : alk. paper)
Subjects: LCSH: Fan wu liu xing. | Philosophy, Chinese—To 221 B.C.
Classification: LCC B126.F3673 .H83 2023 | DDC 181/.11—dc23/eng/20220919
LC record available at https://lccn.loc.gov/2022022713

10 9 8 7 6 5 4 3 2 1

Contents

Preface	vii
A Note on the Translation	xiii

Part I. "All Things Flow into Form"

"All Things Flow into Form": English Translation	3
"All Things Flow into Form": Chinese Transcription	9

Part II. Analysis

1	Solitude	15
2	Sincerity	31
3	"The Heart of Hearts"	43
4	Walking in the Night	63
5	One	79
Concluding Remarks		95
Acknowledgments		111
Notes		113
Index		141

Preface

Let's begin by bringing an imaginary lens into focus. Little by little, we make out a solitary figure. He's standing before a log bridge, which spans a deep abyss. All around is darkness. As he takes his first hesitant step onto the bridge, we zoom in and attempt to look deep into his eyes, searching for that revelatory moment when we might know his true state of mind. Does he waver? Does he wield an inner resolve? Does he stop short and turn back, or does he make it across? This cliffhanger of sorts is where things are left in the *Huainanzi* 淮南子. All we are told in this encyclopedic compendium sponsored by a prince of the second century BCE is that the man's feeling of apprehension was the same regardless of whether or not he was alone.

I will return to this scene later, particularly when I consider a fable from *Xunzi* 荀子 and the traditions behind the name of the protagonist. Different elements of this scene appear in almost every one of the ancient sources that I will discuss in the pages that follow: the journey, the aloneness, the self-scrutiny, the trial. Read on their own, they appear disparate; as a whole they point to a common discourse addressing a real political concern. It is my aim to reconstruct this discourse. I do so through recourse to a newly unearthed document from the Warring States period (481–221 BCE), the "Fan wu liu xing" 凡 (凡) 勿 (物) 流型 (形) or "All Things Flow into Form."

Published by the Shanghai Museum in 2008, the provenance of "All Things Flow into Form" is largely unknown: it was stolen from a tomb, sold on the black market, and subsequently acquired by the museum, where it now sits with close to one hundred texts that hail from at least two different sources.[1] Although the authenticity of the manuscript is sometimes questioned, the controversy may be put to rest by a simple observation: the backs of some of the bamboo slips from the Shanghai Museum collection contain etchings made by a sharp object, intended to facilitate the ordering of the slips. Such physical features also appear in other Warring States manuscripts. This tradition, however, was not known to the scholarly world until Sun Peiyang 孫沛陽 pointed it out in an article published in 2011.[2] Because it would not have been possible for a forger to anticipate Sun's finding and make the etchings before they were recognized as such, this is evidence that the texts from the Shanghai Museum collection are not a forgery. To be sure, the Shanghai Museum collection is not all from one source, and we do not know if such etchings also appear on the back of the slips containing "All Things Flow into Form"; but in the light of this finding, together with other corroborating evidence in both form and content, we may assume the authenticity of these manuscripts until proven otherwise. That is, the burden of proof should lie with those who question the authenticity of these slips, and not with those who accept it.[3]

As such, the text of "All Things Flow into Form" is actually available in two copies, though scholars generally only refer to the first because it is the better preserved of the two. Consisting of thirty bamboo slips, with more than eight hundred characters, it is roughly the length of the text that now opens the *Zhuangzi* 莊子, "Free and Easy Wandering" (Xiaoyao you 逍遙遊). Based on similarities with discoveries that were archaeologically excavated, most scholars date it to the late fourth century BCE, originating in the ancient Chu 楚 region. This is a point to which I will later return as I consider the relation between "All Things Flow into Form" and one of those newly unearthed documents for which more information is available. In terms of its content, "All Things Flow into Form" is divided into two parts: the first is made up almost entirely of questions that concern the origins of Heaven, Earth, and the things of this world; the second is an exposition of the principle of Oneness. Because many of its key words, expressions, and even entire statements can also be found in other ancient texts, any reading of "All Things Flow into Form" should take into consideration these relevant sources, paying special attention to their different nuances despite the overall similarity. Such is the challenge presented by the new discovery that is "All Things Flow into Form." Given the complexity of the approach—one should read the manuscript for what it says, but not in isolation from other ancient texts—we may dwell on this topic a little longer, using the *Zhuangzi* as our example.

For the *Zhuangzi* and many other ancient Chinese texts transmitted throughout the ages, previous scholars have worked to establish their fundamentally composite nature, separate the various chronological strata, and divide them into different textual groupings.⁴ While the precision and persuasiveness of these endeavors vary across the board, they provide a basis of sorts for one's reading of the texts. In the case of the *Zhuangzi*, most scholars agree that the so-called Inner chapters (1–7) constitute the core of the text, even though this analysis is not necessarily correlated with the archaeological evidence: the few ancient manuscript fragments of the *Zhuangzi* that survive actually belong with the "Outer" and "Miscellaneous" chapters.⁵ This is not so much a contradiction as it is a reminder that the circulation of these texts was more complex than previously supposed, and the critical question is not what was early or authentic but who judged it to be early and authentic, when and where that judgment was made, and why. For me, it suffices to understand a work such as the *Zhuangzi* as the writings attributed to and associated with the philosopher by that name (literally, Master Zhuang), dated roughly to the time period with which we are concerned. Apart from that, the focus of my discussion is on the newly discovered document. This is not to suggest that the manuscript constitutes some kind of absolute reality to which all other sources must conform, just that there is great urgency in our making sense of the newly available resource, and this is how I have decided to proceed.

What I propose to do in the following pages, besides offering a full translation of "All Things Flow into Form," is to use particular passages from this work as a way to draw out some of its most interesting features. I divide my analysis into five chapters. The first, "Solitude," sets up the framework of my discussion with a cross-reading of "The Great and Venerable Teacher" (Da zongshi 大宗師) from the *Zhuangzi* and "Far-off Journey" (Yuanyou 遠遊) from *The Songs of the South* (Chuci 楚辭), arguing that a journey in the night and the transformative experience associated with it are key to our understanding of "All Things Flow into Form."

The second and third chapters delve into "All Things Flow into Form" itself, particularly how the discourses surrounding topics such as sincerity (*cheng* 誠)—even if they are not explicitly mentioned in "All Things Flow into Form"—nevertheless inform our reading of this text. In so doing, we may find it helpful to see "All Things Flow into Form" and related discussions as having been embroiled in a debate with the proponents of legalist thought.

In the fourth chapter, I take on the notion of "a walk in the night." After reviewing the different terminologies used to describe this clandestine movement, I turn to Xunzi 荀子 and demonstrate how a fable recorded in the writings of this late Warring States thinker can be read against "All

Things Flow into Form." Indeed, Xunzi's fable might have been intended as a direct criticism against the conception of "the heart of hearts" that is key to this newly discovered manuscript.

In the fifth chapter, "One," I focus on the notion of Oneness that was already introduced in the previous chapter, but I more directly point out that its discussion in "All Things Flow into Form" was intended as an alternative to other prevalent approaches for improving oneself and attaining the Way, particularly divination and physiological exercise. In this way, "All Things Flow into Form" parallels not only the *Zhuangzi* but also discussions in the *Guanzi* 管子 and *Xunzi*. In the conclusion, I take on some remaining topics related to "All Things Flow into Form": its relative date, its literary form, and the broader intellectual theme underlying the text as a whole, namely, the question of a prime mover behind the operations of all things in this world.

These are the figures with whom we will cross paths during the course of this book:

- A poetic persona bemoaning his fate, only to reencounter the fair lady who had once rejected him in the most unlikely of circumstances.

- Two disciples of Confucius, one beaming with life, having even put on some weight in this state of ease and calm, and the other emaciated and anxious because he has yet to "overcome himself."

- Another troubled student, who, upon arriving at Laozi's door after a journey of seven days and seven nights, is startled when asked: "Why did you come with all this crowd of people?"

- An adroit archer who mistakes a rock for a tiger.

- A buffoon who is frightened by his own shadow.

And, in addition to the log bridge spanning the abyss, we will visit:

- The headwaters of the Xia River, where the water is deep and the fish are plenty.

- Ox Mountain, where trees are cut down daily but replenish after a period of rest.

- An empty chamber with a glowing light, which begs the question: if no one is there, then where does the light come from?

A Note on the Translation

"All Things Flow into Form" is available in two versions, A and B. Scholars usually only refer to the former, given that it is better preserved.[1] Since the publication of the manuscript, many proposals have come forward suggesting a different sequence of the thirty slips of version A, and I follow this increasingly accepted consensus, as can be seen in the translation and the original Chinese text that follows. This new sequence divides the text into two halves: a first that resembles a questionnaire, consisting of slips 1–11, 12a + 13b, and 14 and a second, an exposition of the principle of Oneness, consisting of slips 14, 26, 18, 28, 15, 24, 25, 21, 13a + 12b, 22, 23, 17, 19, 20, 29, and 30.[2] The irregular numbering reflects the extent to which the new sequence departs from the decisions of the initial editors. Following standard practices, the Chinese transcription includes a first layer that reflects, on the level of the characters, all the graphic elements of significance as they appear on the bamboo slips and a second (in parentheses) that supplies the equivalents of those characters as more commonly seen in the transmitted literary record. Needless to say, both are heuristic in nature, not intended to replace the photographs of the original bamboo slips so beautifully reproduced in the official publication by the Shanghai Museum.

Several features of the text are worth noting at the outset. The first is the use of the expression *wen zhi yue* 聞之曰 ("It has been said") to introduce a noninterrogative statement. This appears eight times in the text and provides a generally reliable indicator for dividing the text into smaller units, which I mark in the translation by the bamboo slip numbers for each unit (found in parentheses at the end of each unit). As mentioned before, the numbering of these slips is somewhat irregular because they have been rearranged in a new sequence.

xiii

One of these textual units, the section found on slips 2–4, calls for some explanation. Here the expression "It has been said" is followed immediately by several questions rather than the noninterrogative statement found after all other occurrences of the same expression. But later in this section is the statement: 有得而成、未知左右之情、天地立終立始 "It is that, upon being completed, one does not know the reality of what is left and right, or the beginnings and ends as established by Heaven and Earth." I believe this noninterrogative statement is the topic of "It has been said," and the relation between the two has been somewhat obscured by the questions between them. In general, the expression "It has been said" (*wen zhi yue* 聞之曰) contrasts with another expression that also appears in the initial position of a section: *wen* 問 ("It is asked"). This second expression appears only once in the text (the section on slips 11, 12a + 13b, 14), even though one might have expected it in at least two other sections that consist entirely of questions. I would suggest that the function of "It is asked" (*wen* 問) is not to mark all questions in general but to highlight the section where it does appear and distinguish it from those immediately following it. It goes without saying that both *wèn* ("to ask") and *wén* ("to hear") from *wén zhi yue* are etymologically related and form a kind of deictic pair; they are written in the manuscript with the same character and have to be distinguished by context.

Other notable points about the text involve the section on slips 8–11. It begins with the expression "It has been said," followed by the noninterrogative statement: 升高從埤, 至遠從邇 "Ascending high, one starts low; traveling far, one begins near." The discussion continues with several analogies: a tree that grows from small to large, a distance that spans from a single step to thousands of miles. This is followed by a pair of puns: "The sun has an ear, what does it hear? The moon has an army, what does it attack?" Here the play on words involves the homophony or near homophony between "solar prominence" (*er* 珥) and "ear" (*er* 耳) and "lunar halo" (*yun* 暈) and "army" (*jun* 軍).

At the end of this section, we come across two parallel statements: "When the sun first emerges, why is it big but not hot? At noon, why is it small so that one puts on cool clothes?" The first is straightforward enough: 日之始出, 何故大而不炎. The second is more problematic, and my translation is a reconstruction that differs from what appears on the bamboo slips: *其入中, 奚故小而附襜. The details are too technical to be presented here; instead I refer interested readers to my Chinese article on the matter.[3] As I explain there, one of the advantages of reading the text in this modified way is that the word *chan* 襜 (*tham) "cool clothes" rhymes with *yan* 炎 (*lam) from the immediately preceding statement. While it is not necessarily the case that these two statements are parallel and must rhyme with each other, up to this point the rhyming in the text has been fairly consistent, and it is not until the second half of the text, beginning with the section on slips 14, 16, and 26, that it becomes more sporadic and harder to detect.

Finally, a note about the word *xin* 心, which is both a physical organ and a mental faculty, with physiological features that we tend to associate with the heart as well as cognitive capacities that we usually identify in the mind. It is often synonymous with *zhong* 中 and *nei* 內. Both of these words refer to what is internal to oneself, though the former has more of a sense of being embedded in something, whereas the latter is often contrasted with *wai* 外 ("external"). All of them can be "heart" or "mind" as befits the context. In the translation and the rest of this book, I sometimes use "mind," sometimes "heart," but never "heart/mind," increasingly the go-to term for many scholars writing about ancient Chinese intellectual thought, because it seems to me that common parlance allows for a certain looseness in the use of these words. In war propaganda, for example, we say, "winning hearts and minds" as a euphemism for "conquering the minds."

PART 1
"ALL THINGS FLOW INTO FORM"

"All Things Flow into Form"
English Translation

All things flow into form; what brings them to completion?
Flowing forms complete the body; what makes them never die?
Having been completed, having been born, what makes them cry?
Having budded, having taken root, what do they follow, and what do they precede?
The respective abodes of yin and yang, what keeps them stable?
The harmony of water and fire, what keeps them from being at odds? (slips 1–2)

It has been said:
People flow into form; how do they get to be born?
Flowing forms complete the body; how do they lose it and die?
It is that upon being completed, one does not know the reality of what is left and [what is] right, or the beginnings and ends as established by Heaven and Earth.
Heaven sends down the five measures, what makes me know to go up or down?
The five energies arrive in unison, what makes me able to distinguish them?
Among the five teachings of the people, which one is common to all?
For lands beyond the nine territories, who decides their boundaries? (slips 2–4)

When I have grown frail and old, who will serve me?
If ghosts are born from people, for what reason are they
 divinely intelligent?
What makes it that, when flesh and bones have disintegrated,
 their wisdom is even more manifest?
What place do they go upon bidding farewell? Who knows
 their domain?
Ghosts are born from people. What requires me to serve them?
When flesh and bones have disintegrated, their bodies no
 longer visible, why do I feed them?
Their coming and going have no regularity, how do I wait for
 them by the grave?
How do sacrifices reach them? What do I do to satiate them?
In complying with the Way of Heaven, what do I make my
 first priority?
If I want to have harmony among the people, on which
 affairs do I place the greatest weight?
In what way is Heaven's brilliance attained? In what way are
 ghosts fed, numinous as they are? By what means was the
 wisdom of the kings of old so complete? (slips 4–8)

It has been said:
Ascending high, one starts low; traveling far, one begins near.
For a tree of ten armspans, its initial growth is from a shoot.
Feet that are about go a thousand miles must begin with a
 single inch.
The sun has an ear, what does it hear?
The moon has an army, what does it attack?
Water flows eastward, what does it ever fill?
When the sun first emerges, why is it big but not hot?
At noon, why is it small so that one puts on cool clothes?
    (slips 8–11)

It is asked:
How high is Heaven? How expansive is Earth?
What is Heaven? What is Earth?
What are thunder and lightning?
What is the Thearch?
How does soil get to be level? How does water get to be clear?

How do plants get to grow? How do birds and animals get to sing?
When rain falls, who is spitting and sweating it?
When the wind arrives, who is breathing and spreading it? (slips 11, 12A, 13B, 14)

It has been said:
Discerning the Way, one sits and does not descend from the sitting mat.
Wearing the dark sacrificial robe and cap, one makes plans and needs not involve himself in actual affairs.
One knows about the four seas before others, having his hearing extend a thousand miles, and having his vision reach a hundred miles.
Thus, while the sage resides in his home, he is able to know before others the state's perils and prospects, the insurgence of thieves and robbers. (slips 14, 16, 26)

It has been said:
If the mind does not prevail over the mind, then great chaos arises;
If the mind is able to prevail over the mind, this is called "arriving in the morning."
What is meant by "arriving in the morning"? That one reveals oneself for inspection by others.
How is it known that one has revealed himself? That one is at ease with himself for all his life.
Is one capable of speaking few words? Capable of being One? This is called "paring down what is completed."
It is said:
It is only the ruler that the hundred clans value. It is only the mind that the ruler values. It is only One that the mind values.
If it gets to be released, then upward it fills up Heaven, and downward it coils up in the abyss.
Reflecting while one is seated, one plans what is a thousand miles away.
Getting to action as one arises, one displays it to the four seas. (slips 26, 18, 28, 15)

It has been said:

One knows by understanding the reality of things, becomes divine by discerning knowledge, becomes the same by discerning divineness, becomes reserved by discerning sameness, becomes distressed by discerning what has been reserved, and starts over again after discerning distress.

Thus the old is new, people die and go back to being people, and water returns to Heaven.

As a general rule the hundred things do not die, like the moon, which comes out and goes back in, terminates and starts again, arrives and returns.

Examine this teaching, and one can rise up from a single strand. (slips 15, 24, 25)

It has been said:

One begets two, two begets three, three begets four, and four are crisscrossed.

Thus, when there is One, there is nothing in the world that cannot be had; and without it, there is also not one thing in the world that can be had.

Even without one's eyes, one knows its name. Even without one's ears, one hears its sound.

The plants grow on its account; the birds and animals sing because of it.

At a distance, it can be offered to Heaven, and close at hand, to people.

Thus, examination of the Way is the way to cultivate oneself and govern the state. (slips 21, 13A, 12B, 22)

It has been said:

If one is capable of discerning Oneness, then the hundred things will not be lost.

If one is not capable of discerning Oneness, then the hundred things will all be lost.

If one wishes to discern Oneness, look up and one sees it, look down and one manages it. Do not gauge it from afar, but examine it within oneself.

To obtain Oneness and to make plans with it, it is like unifying the world and seizing hold of it.

To obtain Oneness and to contemplate it, it is like unifying the world and ordering it.
One maintains Oneness in order to examine Heaven and Earth.
For this reason, Oneness is tasteful when it is chewed, pungent when it is smelled, sonorous when it is drummed, visible when one draws near, handy when it is handled, but lost when one tries to grasp it, parched when it is ruined, and destroyed when it is cheated.
Examine this teaching, and one can rise up from a single strand. (slips 22, 23, 17, 19, 20)

It has been said:
This one teaching is never exhausted, this one teaching wins the multitude.
This one teaching brings profit to the myriad people, this one teaching enables one to examine Heaven and Earth.
Grasp it, it is too small to hold; spread it out, it can be contained by nothing.
Enlarged, one knows the world with it; and reduced, one orders the state with it. (slips 20, 29, 30)

"All Things Flow into Form"
Chinese Transcription

凡 (凡) 勿 (物) 湍 (流) 型 (形), 系 (奚) 旱 (得) 而 城 (成)? 流型 (形) 城 (成) 豊 (體), 系 (奚) 旱 (得) 而不死? 既城 (成) 既生, 系 (奚) 募 (顧) 而鳴? 既杲 (拔) 既槿 (根), 系 (奚) 逡 (後) 【1】 之系 (奚) 先? 侌 (陰) 易 (陽) 之尻 (處), 系 (奚) 旱 (得) 而固? 水火之和, 系 (奚) 旱 (得) 而不匡 (詭)?

睧 (聞) 之曰: 民人湍 (流) 型 (形), 系 (奚) 旱 (得) 而生? 【2】 湍 (流) 型 (形) 城 (成) 豊 (體), 系 (奚) 遊 (失) 而死? 又 (有) 旱 (得) 而城 (成), 未晢 (知) 左右之請 (情)、天陞 (地) 立冬 (終) 立怠 (始)。天陞 (降) 五尾 (度), 虐 (吾) 系 (奚) 【3】 臭 (衡) 系 (奚) 從 (縱)? 五既 (氣) 竝至, 虐 (吾) 系 (奚) 異系 (奚) 同? 五言才 (在) 人, 箮 (孰) 為之公? 九囟 (域) 出誨 (畝), 箮 (孰) 為之佳 (封)?

虐 (吾) 既長而 【4】 或 (又) 老, 箮 (孰) 為宇 (薦) 奉? 視 (鬼) 生於人, 系 (奚) 古 (故) 神杲 (明)? 骨＝ (骨肉) 之既朿 (靡), 丌 (其) 晢 (智) 愈暲 (彰); 丌 (其) 夬 (訣) 系 (奚) 窐 (適), 箮 (孰) 晢 (知) 【5】 丌 (其) 彊 (彊)? 視 (鬼) 生於人, 虐 (吾) 系 (奚) 古 (故) 事之? 骨＝ (骨肉) 之既朿 (靡), 身豊 (體) 不見, 虐 (吾) 系 (奚) 自飤 (食) 之? 丌 (其) 忞 (來) 亡 (無) 尾 (度), 【6】 虐 (吾) 系 (奚) 旹 (待) 之窒 (窟)? 祭員〈異〉(祀) 系 (奚) 逐, 虐 (吾) 女 (如) 之可 (何) 思 (使) 叞 (飽)? 川 (順) 天之道, 虐 (吾) 系 (奚) 㠯 (以) 為頁 (首)? 虐 (吾) 欲旱 (得) 【7】 百眚 (姓) 之和, 虐 (吾) 系 (奚) 事之敢 (重)? 天之臭 (明) 系 (奚) 旱 (得)? 視 (鬼) 之神系 (奚) 飤 (食)? 先王之晢 (智) 系 (奚) 備?

9

聉 (聞) 之曰: 迚 (升) 【8】高從埤, 至遠從迩 (邇)。十回 (圍) 之木, 丌 (其) 旮 (始) 生女 (如) 蘖 (蘖)。足牆 (將) 至千里, 必從岕 (寸) 旮 (始)。日之又 (有)【9】耳, 牆 (將) 可 (何) 聖 (聽)? 月之又 (有) 軍, 牆 (將) 可 (何) 正 (征)? 水之東流, 牆 (將) 可 (何) 浧 (盈)? 日之旮 (始) 出, 可 (何) 古 (故) 大而不習 (炎)? 丌 (其) 人〈入〉【10】申 (中), 系 (奚) 古 (故) 少 (小) 佳 (附) 暲 (襠) 皷 (褕)?

聉 (問): 天箮 (孰) 高與 (歟)? 陞 (地) 箮 (孰) 裒 (遠) 与 (歟)? 箮 (孰) 為天? 箮 (孰) 為陞 (地)? 箮 (孰) 為靁 (雷)【11】神 (電)? 箮 (孰) 為啻 (帝)? 土系 (奚) 旱 (得) 而坪 (平)? 水系 (奚) 旱 (得) 而清? 卉 (草) 木系 (奚) 旱 (得) 而生?【12A】含 (禽) 獸系 (奚) 旱 (得) 而鳴?【13B】夫雨之至, 箮 (孰) 靁 (唾) 濾 (津) 之? 夫 凸 (風) 之至, 箮 (孰) 虪 (噓) 飄 (吸) 而迸之?

聉 (聞) 之曰: 戠 (察) 道, 坐不下筶 (席); 耑 (端) 曼 (冕)【14】, 箮 (圖) 不旮 (舉) 事, 之〈先〉暂 (知) 四海 (海), 至聖 (聽) 千里, 達見百里。是古 (故) 聖人尿〈尻 (處)〉於丌 (其) 所, 邦家 (家) 之【16】匡 (危) 佞 (安) 廗 (存) 忘 (亡)、惻 (賊) 怸 (盜) 之复 (作), 可之〈先〉暂 (知)。

聉 (聞) 之曰: 心不勅 (勝) 心, 大斲 (亂) 乃复 (作); 心女 (如) 能勅 (勝) 心,【26】是胃 (謂) 少 (朝) 敞 (徹)。系 (奚) 胃 (謂) 少 (朝) 敞 (徹)? 人白為戠 (察)。系 (奚) 呂 (以) 暂 (智) 其白? 冬 (終) 身自若。能彔 (寡) 言虐 (乎)? 能毗 (一)【18】虐 (乎)? 夫此之胃 (謂) 省 (削) 城 (成)。曰: 百酉 (姓) 斎=(之所) 貴唯君= (君,君) 斎=(之所) 貴唯心= (心,心) 斎=(之所) 貴唯毗 (一)。旱 (得) 而解之, 上【28】賽 (塞) 於天, 下番 (蟠) 於困 (淵)。坐而思之, 每 (謀) 於千里; 记 (起) 而用之, 練 (陳) 於四海 (海)。

聉 (聞) 之曰: 至 (致) 情而暂 (知),【15】戠 (察) 暂 (知) 而神, 戠 (察) 神而同,〔察同〕而僉 (斂), 戠 (察) 僉 (斂) 而困, 戠 (察) 困而迬 (復)。氐 (是) 古 (故) 陳為新, 人死迬 (復) 為人, 水迬 (復)【24】於天。凸 (凡) 百勿 (物) 不死女 (如) 月。出惻 (則) 或 (又) 內 (入), 冬 (終) 則或 (又) 詡 (始), 至則或 (又) 反。戠 (察) 此言, 记 (起) 於毗 (一) 耑 (端)。【25】

聉 (聞) 之曰: 毗 (一) 生兩, 兩生厽 (三), 厽 (三) 生女〈四〉, 女〈四〉城 (成) 結。是古 (故) 又 (有) 毗 (一), 天下亡 (無) 不

又 (有);亡 (無) 𦣻 (一), 天下亦亡 (無) 𦣻 (一) 又 (有)。亡 (無)【21】〔目〕而智 (智) 名, 亡 (無) 耳而聏 (聞) 聖 (聲)。卉 (草) 木尋 (得) 之呂 (以) 生, 含 (禽) 獸尋 (得) 之呂 (以) 嗚 (鳴), 遠之坓 (薦)【13A】天, 宓 (近) 之坓 (薦) 人, 是古 (故)【12B】戠 (察) 道, 所呂 (以) 攸 (修) 身而詞 (治) 邦家 (家)。

聏 (聞) 之曰: 能戠 (察) 𦣻 (一), 則百勿 (物) 不遊 (失); 女 (如) 不能戠 (察) 𦣻 (一), 則【22】百勿 (物) 唄 (具) 遊 (失)。女 (如) 欲戠 (察) 𦣻 (一), 卬 (仰) 而見 (視) 之, 符 (俯) 而癸 (揆) 之, 母 (毋) 遠忟 (求) 尾 (度), 於身旨 (稽) 之。尋 (得) 𦣻 (一) 〔而〕【23】 𢝊 (圖) 之, 女 (如) 并天下而獻 (担) 之; 尋 (得) 𦣻 (一) 而思之, 若并天下而詞 (治) 之。肘 (守) 𦣻 (一) 以為天陞 (地) 旨 (稽)。【17】是古 (故) 𦣻 (一), 獻 (咀) 之又 (有) 未 (味), 敤 (嗅) 〔之有臭〕, 鼓之又 (有) 聖 (聽), 忻 (近) 之可見, 操之可鵦 (操), 掾 (握) 之則遊 (失), 敗之則【19】高 (槁), 測 (賊) 之則泧 (滅)。戠 (察) 此言, 迟 (起) 於 𦣻 (一) 耑 (端)。

聏 (聞) 之曰: 𦣻 (一) 言而冬 (終) 不贛 (窮), 𦣻 (一) 言而又 (有) 衆,【20】{衆} 𦣻 (一) 言而萬民之利, 𦣻 (一) 言而為天陞 (地) 旨 (稽)。掾 (握) 之不涅 (盈) 掾 (握), 專 (敷) 之亡 (無) 所舀 〈容〉, 大【29】之呂 (以) 智 (知) 天下, 少 (小) 之呂 (以) 詞 (治) 邦。之力古之力乃下 (?) 上 (?)【30】

PART 2
ANALYSIS

CHAPTER 1

Solitude

The best place to begin a discussion of "All Things Flow into Form" is with a text from the *Zhuangzi* called "The Great and Venerable Teacher" (Da zongshi 大宗師). This is a dialogue between the novice Nanbo Zikui 南伯子葵 and the mysterious but wise Nüyu 女偊.

> 南伯子葵問乎女偊曰:「子之年長矣,而色若孺子,何也?」曰:「吾聞道矣。」南伯子葵曰:「道可得學邪?」曰:「惡!惡可!子非其人也。夫卜梁倚有聖人之才,而无聖人之道;我有聖人之道,而无聖人之才。吾欲以教之,庶幾其果為聖人乎!不然,以聖人之道告聖人之才,亦易矣。吾猶守而告之,參日而後能外天下;已外天下矣,吾又守之,七日而後能外物;已外物矣,吾又守之,九日而後能外生;已外生矣,而後能朝徹;朝徹,而後能見獨;見獨,而後能无古今;无古今,而後能入於不死不生。殺生者不死,生生者不生。其為物,无不將也,无不迎也;无不毀也,无不成也。其名為攖寧。攖寧也者,攖而後成者也。」南伯子葵曰:「子獨惡乎聞之?」曰:「聞之副墨之子,副墨之子聞諸洛誦之孫,洛誦之孫聞之瞻明,瞻明聞之聶許,聶許聞之需役,需役聞之於謳,於謳聞之玄冥,玄冥聞之參寥,參寥聞之疑始。」[1]

Nanbo Zikui asked Nüyu, "You are old, indeed, and yet your complexion is that of a child. Why is this?"

She said, "I have heard the Way!"

Nanbo Zikui said, "Can the Way be learned?"

She said, "Goodness, how could that be? Anyway, you are not the man to do it. Now, there is Buliang Yi—he has the talent of a sage but not the Way of a sage, whereas I have the Way of a sage but not the talent of a sage. I thought I would try to teach him and see if I could really get anywhere near to making him a sage. Otherwise, it would also be easy to explain the Way of a sage to someone who has the talent of a sage. So I kept at him and explained [it] to him for three days, and after that he was able to put the world outside himself. When he had put the world outside himself, I kept at him for seven days more, and after that he was able to put things outside himself. When he had put things outside himself, I kept at him for nine days more, and after that he was able to put life outside himself. After he had put life outside himself, he was able to arrive at dawn. When he had arrived at dawn, he could see his own aloneness. After he had managed to see his own aloneness, he could do away with past and present. After he had done away with past and present, he was able to enter where there is no life and no death. That which kills life does not die; that which gives life to life has never been born. This is the kind of thing it is: there is nothing it does not send off, nothing it does not welcome, nothing it does not destroy, nothing it does not complete. Its name is *ying ning*. *Ying ning* is to 'disturb' [*ying*] and then 'attain completion' [*cheng*]."

Nanbo Zikui asked, "How is it that you alone heard about this?"

She said, "I heard it from the son of Aided-by-Ink, and Aided-by-Ink heard it from the grandson of Repeated-Recitation, and the grandson of Repeated-Recitation heard it from Seeing-Brightly, and Seeing-Brightly heard it from Whispered-Agreement, and Whispered-Agreement heard it from Waiting-for-Use, and Waiting-for-Use heard it from Exclaimed-Wonder, and Exclaimed-Wonder heard it from Dark-Obscurity, and Dark-Obscurity heard it from Participation-in-Mystery, and Participation-in-Mystery heard it from Copy-the-Source."

In Nüyu's dialogue with Nanbo Zikui, she relays her encounter with a third figure, Bu Liangyi 卜梁倚. Since Nüyu herself is knowledgeable about "the Way of a sage" (*shengren zhi Dao* 聖人之道), she instructs this third figure, a promising student who has "the talent of a sage" (*shengren zhi cai* 聖人之才), to advance through the various stages of enlightenment. Several expressions from Nüyu's account are worth explicating. These are "arriving at dawn" (*zhao che* 朝徹), "seeing one's aloneness" (*jian du* 見獨), and most interestingly, *ying ning* 攖寧, which according to Nüyu means something like "disturbing tranquility," but which I believe is more complex than meets the eye. As for the rest of Nüyu's comment, particularly the list of names that Nüyu identifies as her sources on the Way, it is evident that they are a kind of wordplay, intended not to identify any actual people but rather to suggest the futility of any effort to define and pinpoint the Way. Although these names are not uninteresting in themselves, it seems to me that Burton Watson's translation, cited here, is as good as any in making sense of them, and I will largely put them aside in the discussion that follows.

To understand Nüyu's remarks in "The Great and Venerable Teacher," I propose comparing them with several works from the ancient anthology of poetry *The Songs of the South* (Chuci 楚辭). This includes not only "Far-off Journey" (Yuanyou 遠遊) but also several poems written in imitation of it.[2] Beginning with the poetic cycle composed by Liu Xiang 劉向 (79–8 BCE), "Nine Laments" (Jiutan 九嘆), one of the pieces of this poem is called "Saddened by Sufferings" (Youku 憂苦), and it contains the following line about the exile of the poetic persona: 辭九年而不復兮, 獨煢煢而南行 "Nine years now I have left [my native land] without returning. Alone I go on my lonely way to the south."[3] Here the word *qiongqiong* 煢煢 is preceded by *du* 獨 ("alone"), no doubt the reason that the earliest commentator of the anthology, Wang Yi 王逸 (ca. second century CE), glosses it as *dumao* 獨貌 ("the appearance of aloneness"). This can be compared with another line from the anonymous but perhaps earlier "Nine Declarations" (Jiuzhang 九章), in the piece called "Thinking of a Fair One" (Si meiren 思美人). According to this text: 獨煢煢而南行兮, 思彭咸之故也 "Alone, forlorn, I pass on my southward journey, with my thoughts all on Peng Xian bending," where Peng Xian 彭咸 is a figure that recurs throughout "Nine Declarations," and indeed the rest of *The Songs of the South*, as a kind of guiding light to the troubled poet.[4] Although *qiongqiong* 煢煢 is slightly different than *qiongqiong* 煢煢 in "Saddened by Sufferings," the parallel between the two is obvious, as confirmed by the word *du* ("alone") that immediately precedes them. I would connect this with the expression "seeing one's aloneness" (*jian du*) from "The Great and Venerable Teacher."

For another usage of *qiongqiong* 煢煢, we may turn to "Far-off Journey" itself:

遭沈濁而汙穢兮, 獨鬱結其誰語?
夜耿耿而不寐兮, 魂煢煢而至曙。[5]

> Fallen on a time of foulness and impurity, alone with my misery,
>   I had no one to confide in.
> In the night-time I lay, wide-eyed, without sleeping; my unquiet
>   soul was active until the daylight.

Although previous commentators have taken *qiongqiong* in this particular instance to refer to the soul's restlessness (an interpretation followed by David Hawkes in his translation), the meaning of "alone" is hinted by the word *du* not too far ahead. More important are the description of the spirit journey that is so central to this poem and the indication that it takes place at night.[6] Note the parallel between the suggestion that the soul remained active "until the daylight" (*zhi shu* 至曙), on the one hand, and *zhao che* "arriving at dawn" from "The Great and Venerable Teacher," on the other. As we will soon see in "Far-off Journey," all the discomfiture that accompanies one's sleeplessness at night will quickly transform into enlightenment, perhaps because one has persisted through the ordeal and come to the other end of the tunnel, so to speak. This is the second connection that I would like to make between the two texts.

Throughout his journey, the poetic persona of "Far-off Journey" reflects on the limits of life and senses a feeling of isolation:

> 惟天地之無窮兮，哀人生之長勤；
> 往者余弗及兮，來者吾不聞。

> I thought of the limitless vastness of the universe; I wept for
>   the long affliction of man's life.
> Those that had gone before I should never see; and those yet
>   to come I should never know of.

As the journey continues and his loneliness grows, this feeling does not erupt in any emotional outburst. Instead, his mind undergoes a transformation as he finds equanimity:

> 內惟省以端操兮，求正氣之所由；
> 漠虛靜以恬愉兮，澹無為而自得。

> Then I looked into myself to strengthen my resolution, and
>   sought to learn from where the primal spirit issues.
> In emptiness and silence I found serenity; in tranquil inaction
>   I gained true satisfaction.

I will return later to such expressions as "inaction" (*wuwei* 無為) and "self-satisfaction" (*zi de* 自得). Here I will draw attention to the description of his isolation: 往者余弗及兮, 來者吾不聞 "Those that had gone before I should never see; and those yet to come I should never know of." We may compare this with "The Great and Venerable Teacher" and its suggestion that one who has "arrived at dawn" and "seen one's aloneness" is then able to "do away with past and present" (*wu gujin* 无古今), such that "there is nothing he does not send off, nothing he does not welcome" (*wu bu jiang ye, wu bu ying ye* 无不將也, 无不迎也). If the poet was previously anxious about his isolation from past and future, then in his moment of self-realization he learns to put this anxiety aside and come to terms with his aloneness. This is the final connection I would make with the "The Great and Venerable Teacher."

In the overall context of *The Songs of the South*, "Far-off Journey" stands in contrast to "On Encountering Trouble" (Lisao 離騷) and many of the poems cited in this chapter. All of them betray a self-lamenting undertone as the poetic persona reflects on his situation, feeling alone, isolated, and understood by no one. This is a familiar setup about the loyal minister who has been ignored by his ruler and maligned by his colleagues, and "On Encountering Trouble" is one of the earliest and most prominent entries in the tradition. Even as the persona embarks on a spirit journey, he never completely leaves behind this world. His frustration only grows as his experiences in the human and spiritual realms mirror each other and become increasingly similar.

By contrast, in "Far-off Journey," the mood is very different. While this poem begins in the same self-lamenting tone, somberness quickly turns into glee as the persona sets off on his spirit journey. There is a sense of elation, even ecstasy, following each encounter along the way, and the journey ends with the same promise of enlightenment as made by "The Great and Venerable Teacher." In this way, one comes away from "Far-off Journey" with an understanding very different from the rest of *The Songs of the South*. The purpose of the self-lament is no longer the deploring of one's circumstances but the building up of a climactic release that will emancipate the persona from the present and unite him with the forces of the cosmos, transcending both time and space. As described in the final line of this poem: 超無為以至清兮, 與泰初而為鄰 "Transcending Inaction, I came to purity, and entered the neighborhood of the Great Beginning."

Consider the following account from "On Encountering Trouble," an episode from the spirit journey, where the poetic persona is seeking to pass through Heaven's gate (*Changhe* 閶闔): 吾令帝閽開關兮, 倚閶闔

而望予 "I asked Heaven's porter to open up for me; but he leant across Heaven's gate and eyed me churlishly."⁷ Thus denied, he lingers about in a dark mood, reflecting on his experiences in the world below: 時曖曖其將罷兮, 結幽蘭而延佇; 世溷濁而不分兮, 好蔽美而嫉妒 "The day was getting dark and drawing to its close. Knotting orchids, I waited in indecision. The muddy, impure world, so undiscriminating, seeks always to hide beauty, out of jealousy." Ultimately, he carries on and continues with his journey, only to be overwhelmed by an outburst of emotion as he realizes that he is completely alone: 朝吾將濟於白水兮, 登閬風而緤馬; 忽反顧以流涕兮, 哀高丘之無女 "I decided when morning came to cross the White Water, and climbed the peak of Langfeng, and there tied up my steeds. Then I looked about me and suddenly burst out weeping, because on that high hill there was no fair lady." His search for a companion is futile.

In contrast to this, "Far-off Journey" contains a very similar description about the persona's effort to enter Heaven: 命天閽其開關兮, 排閶闔而望予 "I bade Heaven's porter open his barrier, and stand by his gate awaiting my arrival." Here the response by the porter is described with the same word as in "On Encountering Trouble," *wang* 望, but it is "eyeing" with a greater sense of welcome, hence Hawkes's less literal translation "awaiting." Indeed, the persona makes his entrance, and the accompaniment by a spirit in the clouds suggests that he is far from being alone: 召豐隆使先導兮, 問大微之所居; 集重陽入帝宮兮, 造旬始而觀清都 "I summoned Feng Long; I made him ride ahead and ask the way to the Palace of Mystery. Passing through the Bright Walls I entered the House of God, visited the Week Star and gazed on the Pure City."⁸

Consider also the following work by Sima Xiangru 司馬相如 (ca. 179–117 BCE), "Exposition Poem on the Mighty One" (Daren fu 大人賦). Long recognized as having a close relation with "Far-off Journey," this poem contains another variation of the same theme: 排閶闔而入帝宮兮, 載玉女而與之歸 "They batter at the gates of Heaven, enter the palace of the Celestial Emperor, and invite the goddess Jade Maiden to return in their chariots."⁹ Here, the subject is the persona and an entourage that consists of various deities. A comparison with "On Encountering Trouble" and "Far-off Journey" reveals that it is a condensed version of those two poems: not only does the persona go straight to the palace of the Celestial Emperor, but he brings back the same Jade Maiden that he only expected to find, but never did, during his journey in "On Encountering Trouble." Placed side by side, we might say that both "Far-off Journey" and "Exposition Poem on the Mighty One" make an effort to improve upon the sorry fate of the same persona from "On Encountering Trouble."[10]

The poem "Far-off Journey" is often dated rather late by scholars, perhaps the second half of the second century BCE, and associated with Liu An 劉安 (d. 122 BCE), the prince of Huainan who is also responsible for commissioning the *Huainanzi*.[11] While this might be true of its final composition, it is clear that the poem also contains traditions traceable to earlier times—though exactly how early is not easy to say. In terms of "The Great and Venerable Teacher," the assumed author, Zhuangzi the man, is traditionally said to have been active during the fourth century BCE.[12] This is roughly the same period as "All Things Flow into Form." Though unprovenanced, scholars generally place it in the same century based on its similarity with other manuscripts with clearer dates. This gives a time range for us to plot the different sources discussed here.

In anticipation of a major theme for the present study, also one of the most prominent features of "All Things Flow into Form," I would like to draw attention to the interest in the notion of Oneness that is also evident in "Far-off Journey." This appears roughly halfway through the poem, in a series of mostly tetrasyllabic phrases. In a discussion that would not be unfamiliar to readers of the *Laozi* 老子, "Far-off Journey" suggests the following:

道可受兮, 不可傳; 其小無內兮, 其大無垠;
毋滑而魂兮, 彼將自然; 壹氣孔神兮, 於中夜存;
虛以待之兮, 無為之先; 庶類以成兮, 此德之門。

The Way can only be received, it cannot be given.
Small, it has no content; great, it has no bounds.
Keep your soul from confusion, and it will come naturally.
By unifying essence, strengthen the spirit; preserve it inside you
 in the midnight hour.
Await it in emptiness, before even Inaction.[13]
All other things proceed from this: this is the Door of Power.

Surely it is not an accident that these lines of "Far-off Journey" begin with the claim about the ineffability of the Way and end with a reference to the "Door of Power" (*de zhi men* 德之門). This is precisely what one finds in the famous opening lines of the first chapter of the *Laozi*: 道可道, 非常道; 名可名, 非常名 "The way that can be spoken of is not the constant way; the name that can be named is not the constant name," and at the end of the same chapter, the reference to the constant way as *zhongmiao zhi men* 眾妙之門 ("the gateway of the manifold secrets").¹⁴ For our purpose here, what is most interesting is the suggestion by "Far-off Journey" that it is through this door, or the Way, that "all things are completed" (*shulei yi cheng* 庶類以成). This is the literal understanding of the line translated by Hawkes as "all other things proceed from this," and it bears a striking resemblance to the opening of "All Things Flow into Form," including the very first question raised in this text: 凸 (凡) 勿 (物) 湍 (流) 型 (形), 系 (奚) 旱 (得) 而城 (成)? "All things flow into form; what brings them to completion?" As we will see, for our text from the Shanghai Museum, there is a clear answer for what is the driving force behind the creation and completion of all things: it is not the Way, but the principle of Oneness. And this corresponds to the suggestion by "Far-off Journey" to "unify essence" (*yi qi* 壹氣), an expression that echoes an earlier line in the same poem: 見王子而宿之兮, 審壹氣之和德 "There I saw Master Wang and made him salutation, and asked about the balance made by unifying essence."¹⁵ What this suggests for "Far-off Journey" is that it is merging two concepts, the Way and One, emphasized by the opening chapter of the *Laozi* and "All Things Flow into Form," respectively.

It remains for me to go over some remaining examples of *qiongqiong* in *The Songs of the South*. The first is from another piece of "Nine Declarations" called "The Outpouring of Sad Thoughts" (Chou si 抽思):

曾不知路之曲直兮, 南指月與列星;
願徑逝而未得兮, 魂識路之營營。
何靈魂之信直兮, 人之心不與吾心同！¹⁶

> And because it does not know the twists and turns of the way [to Ying], it takes the moon and stars as guides to lead it southwards.
> Thinking to fly straight there; but still it can never reach it and flies distractedly, weaving this way and that.¹⁷
> Why should my soul be so true and constant? The hearts of other men are not the same as my heart.

Here the key word is the reduplicative binome *yingying* 營營 (*weŋ-weŋ), and I would regard it as another written form of *qiongqiong* (*gweŋ-gweŋ), since *ying* 營 is given for *qiong* 煢 in one edition of "Far-off Journey," according to Wang Yi. Under "The Outpouring of Sad Thoughts" itself, Wang notes that one text has *qiong* 煢 in the place of *ying*.¹⁸ Consider

Wang Yi's paraphrase of the last part of the line: 精靈主行, 往來數也 "The essential spirit leads the motion, and it goes to and fro many times." This is based on the *Book of Odes*, where *yingying* is also attested and is glossed by the ancient commentator surnamed Mao 毛 (ca. Warring States) as "the appearance of going to and fro" (*wanglai mao* 往來貌).[19] This is a meaning I would reject in the context of "The Outpouring of Sad Thoughts" due to the connection that I have just made with *qiongqiong*, but then I do not think Wang Yi's paraphrase is far off the mark, either, for "going to and fro" is also a sense implicit in *qiongqiong*, as can be seen in "Far-off Journey" and its emphasis on movement ("those that had gone before I should never see; and those yet to come I should never know of"). Note that *yingying* in "The Outpouring of Sad Thoughts" once again describes a journey in the night, with the reference to the moon and the stars. Earlier in the piece, the poet compares himself to a bird from the south:

有鳥自南兮, 來集漢北。
好姱佳麗兮, 牉獨處此異域。
既惸獨而不群兮, 又無良媒在其側。

There is a bird from the South Country
Come to settle north of the Han;
Most fair and rare and beautiful,
Forlorn he sits in this foreign land,
Alone and cut off from the rest of the flock
With no one by to find him a mate.

With such words as *du* ("forlorn") and *qiongdu* 惸獨 ("alone"), the poet comments on his own solitude. In fact, the latter expression consists of, on the one hand, *qiong* 惸, yet another way of writing *qiongqiong*, now in its monosyllabic form, and on the other, its synonymous counterpart, *du*. In this way, all the themes that I have mentioned with respect to "The Great and Venerable Teacher" can be found in "The Outpouring of Sad Thoughts," if somewhat indirectly: the discussion of aloneness, the journey in the night, the motion of going to and fro. Of course, these themes also appear in "Far-off Journey."

Another example of *qiongqiong* is from "Alas That My Lot Was Not Cast" (Ai shiming 哀時命) by Zhuang Ji 莊忌 (ca. 150 BCE):

魂眰眰以寄獨兮, 汨徂往而不歸;
處卓卓而日遠兮, 志浩蕩而傷懷。[20]

> On and on my soul speeds, seeking a lonely dwelling; swiftly it goes forth, never to return. Aloft and aloft we go, ever more distant, till my mind is unsettled and my heart repines.

With *zhengzheng* 啀啀, one finds in these lines yet another reduplicative binome, but the context of a journey and the occurrence of the word *du* make it clear that this is merely another form of *qiongqiong*; note Wang Yi's gloss of the binome as "the appearance of walking alone" (*duxing mao* 獨行貌). In fact, comparing the sounds of *qiongqiong* (*gweŋ-gweŋ) and *zhengzheng* (*teŋ-teŋ),[21] one notices a contrast between a velar and dental initial, the same as what one finds between *ying* 攖 (*ʔeŋ) and *ning* 寧 (*nên) in the expression *ying ning* ("disturbing tranquility") from "The Great and Venerable Teacher." It is to this expression that our discussion now turns, starting with its sound.

Both *ying* 攖 (*ʔeŋ) and *ning* 寧 (*nên) belong to the Old Chinese rhyme group *geng* 耕, and, if analyzed as a reduplicative like *zhengzheng*, *yingying*, or *qiongqiong* (all of which also happen to be in the same rhyme group), would make up what is traditionally called a "rhyming binome."[22] While such "fission reduplication" (in the terminology of Sun Jingtao 孫景濤) is not completely the same as totally reduplicated words like *qiongqiong*, we may trace them to the same origin, if not actually equate them. For a parallel example, consider *chuoyue* 汋約 (*diauk-ʔiauk), another rhyming binome attested in *The Songs of the South*. In Wang Yi's discussion of the same word, this is given as *chuochuo* 汋汋 (*diauk-diauk).[23] In the same way, *bifei* 蔽芾 (*bjets-pjut) is an alliterative binome—so named due to the similarity of the initials—seen in the *Book of Odes*. It is also quoted as *bibi* 蔽蔽 (*bjets-bjets) in the earliest graphic dictionary, *Explaining Graphs and Analyzing Characters* (*Shuowen jiezi* 說文解字).[24]

By analyzing *yingning* as a reduplicative related to *qiongqiong* in both sound and meaning—and it is entirely possible that they are the same word—we can read the progress in self-cultivation such as described in "The Great and Venerable Teacher" as parallel to the spirit journey in "Far-off Journey" and other poems from *The Songs of the South*. Because "The Great and Venerable Teacher" makes a deliberate attempt to define the meaning of *yingning*, it would have constituted an attempt, already during the Warring States, to explicate the language that is also reflected in that Chu anthology of poetry. In my understanding, one begins the process of self-cultivation by turning inward, by "putting the world outside oneself" (*wai tianxia* 外天下), "putting things outside oneself" (*wai wu* 外物), and "putting life outside oneself" (*wai sheng* 外生). Such actions result in one's absolute solitude, as suggested by the expression *jian du* ("seeing one's aloneness"), but it is also accompanied by an enlightenment that is indicated by the expression *zhao che* ("arriving at dawn"). In this ideal state, the sage transcends past and present, life and death, and maintains a certain equilibrium with the myriad things. All of this is centered on the word *yingning*, the definition of which the "The Great and Venerable Teacher" leaves until the end of the discussion.

There are multiple possibilities why this is the case, none of them mutually exclusive. One is that reduplicatives by nature are elusive and not easy to define; the meaning of *yingning* might have already seemed obscure by the time of "The Great and Venerable Teacher," thus requiring comment from the author of that *Zhuangzi* text. Another possibility is "The Great and Venerable Teacher" was imposing its own take onto a word that was previously understood quite differently. Finally, we have to take into account wordplay; perhaps "The Great and Venerable Teacher" was playing on the literal meanings of the characters used to write the reduplicative binome. Recall the following analysis: 攖寧也者, 攖而後成者也 "*Ying ning* is to 'disturb' [*ying*] and then 'attain completion' [*cheng*]." By glossing *ning* 寧 (*nên) as *cheng* 成 (*deŋ), "The Great and Venerable Teacher" is not only drawing a connection between the two words in terms of their sound (*cheng* is yet another word from the same traditional rhyme group) but also echoing a statement immediately preceding it about the stage at which one has arrived toward the end of one's cultivation process: 无不毀也, 无不成也 "There is nothing it does not destroy, nothing it does not complete." In the same way, the word *hui* 毀 ("to destroy") from this last formulation is parallel to *ying* ("to disturb") from *ying ning*.[25] All of this being said, it remains the case that *ying ning* as a verb-verb construction is awkward, unusual, and nowhere else attested. This is the same kind of stretch in meaning that one finds in Yan Zhitui's 顏之推 (531–ca. 591 CE) reanalysis of the alliterative binome *youyu* 猶豫 ("hesitant") as a dog (*you* 猶) running ahead of its master, thus "anticipating" (*yu* 豫) that person.[26] The only difference is that *yingning* as understood by "The Great and Venerable Teacher" anticipates *youyu* by several centuries, suggesting that such reanalysis can be found as early as the Warring States. Besides dismissing it as untenable or implausible from the perspective of modern linguistics, the more interesting question is what led a particular author or scholar to understand a word in this way, with rationales that are specific to a time and place.

For another example of this kind of reanalysis, closer in time to "The Great and Venerable Teacher," we may consider the case of *weiyi* 逶迤, a reduplicative meaning "winding," "free-flowing," or "at ease." This word is widely attested in the literary record and is variously written as 委它, 委佗, 委陀, 委蛇, having no fewer than twenty forms.²⁷ One instance of this can be found in a text from the *Zhuangzi* called "Perfect Happiness" (Zhile 至樂). In a discussion of birds, the interlocutor points out that a bird should be set free rather than forced to endure the rites and other human activities:

> 夫以鳥養養鳥者, 宜栖之深林, 遊之壇陸, 浮之江湖, 食之鰌鰷, 隨行列而止, 委蛇而處。²⁸

> If you want to nourish a bird with what nourishes a bird, then you should let it roost in the deep forest, play among the banks and islands, float on the rivers and lakes, eat mudfish and minnows, follow the rest of the flock in flight and rest, and live any way it chooses.

Here, "anywhere it chooses" is Watson's translation of the reduplicative *weiyi*, as is consistent with customary usage. Interestingly, in a close parallel to this anecdote, found in another text from the *Zhuangzi*, "Mastering Life" (Da sheng 達生), the same statement appears in a slightly different form:

> 若夫以鳥養養鳥者, 宜棲之深林, 浮之江湖, 食之以委蛇, 則平陸而已矣。²⁹

> If you want to nourish a bird with what will nourish a bird, you had best let it roost in the deep forest, float on the rivers and lakes, and live on snakes—then it can feel at ease.

The same word *weiyi* appears in this second passage, but here reanalyzed as a construction consisting of a modifier and a noun: literally, "serpentine snake." The distinction between these two passages is similar to that between my understanding of *yingning* and the definition given in "The Great and Venerable Teacher." What this shows is that such "mistaken" analysis was practiced not only by the commentators of the Han and later times but also by the authors of the *Zhuangzi*.³⁰ It is possible that "Mastering Life" and "The Great and Venerable Teacher" are making a pun on words such as *weiyi* or *yingning*. This is a kind of playfulness that would not be unexpected from the *Zhuangzi*.³¹

Finally, before leaving behind "The Great and Venerable Teacher" and *The Songs of the South*, I would like to draw attention to the *Mengzi* 孟子, or the teachings attributed to Mencius that are roughly contemporaneous with the earliest layers of *Zhuangzi*. This is the famous discussion of Ox Mountain in the *Mengzi* 6A8.[32]

In Mencius's discussion of human nature and the grave consequences of one who "lets go of his true heart" (*fang qi liangxin* 放其良心), which he compares to axes felling the trees of Ox Mountain, he evokes the notion of "air in the night" (*yeqi* 夜氣). It is through this regenerative energy and the respite in the night that one wakes up to a new day, fully repaired and replenished, even though the new day will also bring about more wear and tear. For Mencius, such a process illustrates the human capacity to constantly reform itself, an indication of our basic inclination to be good. Interestingly, this process also corresponds to the spirit journey described in "Far-off Journey." In both cases, the night marks a time of renewal and rebirth, a transformative process whereby one inches closer to the ideal prescribed by those texts. This is no doubt why "Far-off Journey" gives the following instruction about the night:

毋滑而魂兮, 彼將自然; 壹氣孔神兮, 於中夜存。[33]

Keep your soul from confusion, and it will come naturally.
By unifying your essence, strengthen the spirit; preserve it inside
 you in the midnight hour.

Here, the discussion points to a concern with self-cultivation that echoes "The Great and Venerable Teacher." It is also a theme explicitly stated in many of the texts considered in the following chapter, including "All Things Flow into Form."

In his reference to the notion of "air in the night," It is evident Mencius is alluding to a physiological basis for self-cultivation that is elaborated upon more fully in "Far-off Journey." For further evidence that this physiological basis was more widely shared among ancient authors, we may turn to one of the dialogues from the "Ten Questions" (Shiwen 十問), a medical text excavated from the Han tomb at Mawangdui 馬王堆, Hunan Province (dated shortly after 168 BCE). In it, there appears a discussion of an "old vapor" (*xiuqi* 宿氣) that dissipates in the night, in contrast to a "new vapor" (*xinqi* 新氣) that gathers at dawn. Such reshuffling of *qi* from night to dawn corresponds to the transformative experience described in both Mencius and "Far-off Journey." Just as both of those sources speak of "preserving" (*cun* 存) the *qi* during the night, "Ten Questions" describes releasing this energy at dawn and replacing it with new energy. According to "Ten Questions" (slips 30–32):

> 息必探 (深) 而久, 新氣易〈易〉守。宿氣為老, 新氣為壽。善治氣者, 使宿氣夜散, 新氣朝冣 (最), 以彀 (徹) 九徼 (竅), 而實六府。[34]

> Breathing must be deep and long, so that the new vapor is easy to hold. The old vapor causes aging, the new vapor causes longevity. He who is skilled at cultivating vapor lets the old vapor disperse at night and the new vapor gather at dawn, thereby penetrating the nine apertures and filling the six palaces.

In fact, later in the same text, there are more detailed instructions for breathing at night (slips 37–38):

> 莫 (暮) 息之志, 深息長徐, 使耳勿聞, 且以安寢 (寢)。云 (魂) 柏 (魄) 安刑 (形), 故能長生。夜半之息也, 覺悟 (寤) 毋變寢刑 (形), 探 (深) 余 (徐) 去埶 (勢), 六府皆發, 以長為極。將欲壽神, 必以奏 (腠) 理息。

> The aim of dusk breathing is to breathe deeply, long and slow, causing the ears to not hear, and to sleep soundly. The ethereal-spirit and earthly-spirit are at ease in the form, and this enables one to live long. As for breathing at midnight, upon waking up, do not change your sleeping posture. Do it deeply and slowly, without exertion, the six palaces all open, and make long duration your ideal. If you wish to make the spirit long-lived, you must breathe with the skin's webbed pattern.

Here, one finds the same reference to the six organs of the body serving as a repository of *qi*, or the "six palaces" (*liufu* 六府). Just as one is urged to breathe naturally, not exerting oneself in any way, longevity is attained by breathing with "the skin's webbed pattern," which opens oneself up for the absorption of new *qi*. Once again, it is through a breathing exercise prescribed for the nighttime that one can transform oneself and emerge newly afresh for the start of another day. This is consistent with both Mencius and "Far-off Journey."[35]

We are now ready to turn to "All Things Flow into Form." By reading the "The Great and Venerable Teacher" from the *Zhuangzi* against *The Songs of the South*, particularly "Far-off Journey," I hope to have shown the high degree of correspondence between the two in their account of the process of self-cultivation. This provides a basis for our reading of "All Things Flow into Form." As we will see, there are close parallels between "The Great and Venerable Teacher" and "All Things Flow into Form," both in form and content. Indeed, they share not only some of the same technical terms but also the effort to explicate them. These connections permit us to proceed with the assumption that they all belong to the same intellectual context. They are our first clues to uncovering the mystery of the unprovenanced text that is "All Things Flow into Form."

CHAPTER 2

Sincerity

We turn now to a passage at the heart of "All Things Flow into Form," which is, if not the most important, then certainly the most problematic. As is customary with other parts of "All Things Flow into Form," this passage begins with the formulaic expression, "It has been said." This is followed by the formulation that I refer to as "the heart of hearts," here phrased in the negative: "If the mind does not prevail over the mind." The consequence is spelled out as the following (slips 26, 18, 28, 15):

聞 (聞) 之曰: 心不勅 (勝) 心, 大䛊 (亂) 乃复 (作); 心女 (如) 能勅 (勝) 心, 是胃 (謂) 少 (朝) 敢 (徹)。系 (奚) 胃 (謂) 少 (朝) 敢 (徹)? 人白為戠 (察)。系 (奚) 㠯 (以) 晉 (知) 其白? 冬 (終) 身自若。能募 (寡) 言虗 (乎)? 能𣎳 (一) 虗 (乎)? 夫此之胃 (謂) 省 (削) 城 (成)。曰: 百眚 (姓) 斦= (之所) 貴唯君= (君, 君) 斦= (之所) 貴唯心= (心, 心) 斦= (之所) 貴唯𣎳 (一)。尋 (得) 而解之, 上賽 (塞) 於天, 下番 (蟠) 於困 (淵)。坐而思之, 每 (謀) 於千里; 记 (起) 而用之, 練 (陳) 於四海 (海)。

It has been said: if the mind does not prevail over the mind, then great chaos arises; if the mind is able to prevail over the mind, this is called "arriving in the morning." What is meant by "arriving in the morning"? That one reveals oneself for inspection by others. How is it known that one has revealed himself? That one is at ease with himself for all his life. Is one capable of speaking few words? Capable of being One? This is called "paring down what is completed." It is said: it is only the ruler that the hundred clans value. It is only the mind that the ruler values. It is only One that the mind values. If it gets to be released, then upward it fills up Heaven, and downward it coils up in the abyss. Reflecting while one is seated, one plans what is a thousand miles away. Getting to action as one arises, one displays it to the four seas.

As in the passage from "The Great and Venerable Teacher" of the *Zhuangzi*, considered in the previous chapter, the discussion here proceeds by way of introducing and defining a series of expressions. They consist of the following:

1. 心不勝心:"If the mind does not prevail over the mind"

2. 朝徹:"Arriving at dawn"

3. 人白為察:"Revealing oneself for inspection by others"

4. 終身自若:"To be at ease with oneself for all one's life"

5. 削成:"Paring down what is completed"

Readers will immediately notice that I am reading *zhao che* 朝徹 ("arriving at dawn") for *shao che* 少徹 from "All Things Flow into Form," and the basis for this is, of course, "The Great and Venerable Teacher."[1] The present chapter focuses on why this is so, though I will have occasion to touch on all of the other expressions.

In terms of its content, the passage from "All Things Flow into Form" is concerned with the mind: to isolate it from distractions arising within the mind itself, so an innermost core could be, in a sense, quarantined. Such concern is also seen in "The Great and Venerable Teacher," with its emphasis on "putting the world outside oneself" (*wai tianxia*), "putting things outside oneself" (*wai wu*), and "putting life outside oneself" (*wai sheng*); we could compare more generally *The Songs of the South*, where the poetic persona embarks on his spirit journey, making an effort to leave behind all his worries for this world. These may be the "great chaos" (*daluan* 大亂) rejected by "All Things Flow into Form."

The passage from "All Things Flow into Form" continues with the definition of *zhao che* as *ren bai wei cha* 人白為察 ("revealing oneself for inspection by others"). Here the word *bai* 白 is literally "white," "pure," or "plain." Used nominally, it can refer to a kind of brilliance or glow; verbally, it is "to manifest" or "to reveal," whether this is done through words or deeds. Such an action always assumes the observation of others. Indeed, for "All Things Flow into Form," this observation is explicitly indicated by the word *cha* 察 ("to discern"), and it is reinforced by the later question: 奚以知其白 "How is it known that one has revealed himself?" In other words, with *ren bai wei cha*, I am behaving in a way that I assume I could be seen by a second party. It does not matter whether that second party is actually present, or, in fact, whether that second party is actually "I"—one part of me looking on at another part.[2] In light of the discussion in the previous chapter, we can see how this revelation is the result of one's having "arrived at dawn," since it is in broad daylight that one is most visible. This is the reason that "All Things Flow into Form" goes on to discuss the term *zi ruo* 自若 ("to be at ease with oneself"), which describes the level of comfort that comes from my having nothing to hide and laying everything out in the open. Recall the line from "Far-off Journey": 漠虛靜以恬愉兮, 澹無為而自得 "In emptiness and silence I found serenity; in tranquil inaction I gained true satisfaction." The equanimity described by *zi de* 自得 ("self-satisfaction") belongs to the person who is not attracted—indeed, possessed—by forces and objects on the outside; he is only himself, plain and simple.

Finally, in the last part of the passage, "All Things Flow into Form" evokes the expression *xiao cheng* 削成 ("paring down what is completed"). By prefacing this discussion with the rhetorical questions 能寡言乎, 能一乎 "Is one capable of speaking few words? Capable of being One?" the passage is defining *xiao cheng* as both "one" and "speaking few words." It is interesting to compare this discussion with another newly excavated text, "Grand One Gives Birth to Water" (Taiyi sheng shui 太一生水).[3] As presently constituted, this Warring States manuscript from Guodian 郭店 consists of two different sections. The first, slips 1 through 8, presents a cosmogonic account with "Grand One" (Taiyi 太一) at its center. The second, slips 9 through 14, contains a discussion of a sage who acts according to the Way of Heaven. In spite of all his success, the sage maintains a low profile and takes no credit to his name, adhering to the ideal of "weakness" (*ruo* 弱) favored by the Way of Heaven. As defined by "Grand One Gives Birth to Water": 雀 (削) 城 (成) 者吕 (以) 嗌 (益) 生者 "This is paring down what is completed to enhance life," where 雀城, despite being written differently, parallels 省城 from "All Things Flow into Form." I believe both should read *xiao cheng* ("paring down what is completed"). Note how the theme of "weakness" or humility in "Grand One Gives Birth to Water" echoes the rhetorical questions from "All Things Flow into Form." "Is one capable of speaking few words?" corresponds to the rejection of fame in "Grand One Gives Birth to Water." "Is one capable of being One?" evokes the notion of Oneness that is at the center of the same text. As I will argue by the end of this study, there is one more parallel between "All Things Flow into Form" and "Grand One Gives Birth to Water." Both texts have a bifurcated structure in that one part poses a question and the other supplies an answer. This will prove crucial for dating "All Things Flow into Form."[4]

Throughout this entire passage, "All Things Flow into Form" is discussing several ethical questions of the utmost importance. Can I overcome those forces within me that obstruct the recognition of my true self? Can I be so pure in the mind that I can open myself up for the inspection of others? Can I do so without contrivance and artifice? In raising them, "All Things Flow into Form" is describing a process of introspection where I am solely responsible for myself. Recall the expression *jian du* ("seeing one's aloneness") from "The Great and Venerable Teacher" of the *Zhuangzi* and other related expressions from *The Songs of the South*. One particular manifestation of this, the notion of a journey in the night and the transformative experience taking place during that period, has already been encountered in the previous chapter and will be the pursued further in chapter 4. In terms of the formulation of "the heart of hearts," which I believe is at the very center of this passage, this and other related texts will be the subject of the following chapter. For all these discussions, what is most important is that following one's introspection, a person emerges renewed and much improved. This is the path to moral self-cultivation that we frequently encounter in the teachings of Confucius and other ancient thinkers, but the discussion here allows us to imagine the details of how it takes place: alone, submerged in darkness, with a deep, meditative look into the heart.

In the literary record, the path to moral self-cultivation is sometimes discussed in connection with the term *cheng* 誠 ("sincerity"). To be sure, this term appears nowhere in "All Things Flow into Form," and this is consistent with evidence from the Guodian corpus to which "Grand One Gives Birth to Water" belongs. Despite using a language that closely mirrors the discussion of *cheng*—for instance, the reference to *sheng* 聖 ("sageness") in the "Five Conducts" (Wuxing 五行) and *zhong* 忠 ("loyalty") and *xin* 信 ("trustworthiness") in "The Way of Loyalty and Trustworthiness" (Zhongxin zhi dao 忠信之道)—the Guodian texts do not mention that particular term. Then, too, the evidence from "Doctrine of the Mean" (Zhongyong 中庸) is significant in this regard. As it is generally acknowledged by scholars since

Zhu Xi 朱熹 (1130–1200), this text is made of several textual groupings, and the discussion of *cheng*—important as it is—only turns up in one part of the text, perhaps a later chronological layer.[5]

Where does the notion of *cheng* come from? While the term already appears in the writings attributed to Mencius, it is confined to only two passages in the entire corpus of the *Mengzi*: 4A12 and 7A4 (not counting the use of the word as an adverb meaning "truly"), suggesting that it has only a marginal place in the overall context of Mencius's teachings.[6] Whereas 7A4 is quite brief and appears in the fragmentary "Book Seven," also the last of the seven books of the *Mengzi*, 4A12 evokes the term but goes on to place its emphasis somewhere else.[7] By contrast, in the writings associated with Xunzi, *cheng* appears right at the center and is assigned an importance only paralleled by "Doctrine of the Mean" (and "Great Learning" or Daxue 大學).[8] What this suggests is that the notion arose sometime between Mencius and Xunzi, perhaps early enough so it touched upon the margins of the tradition surrounding that former figure. In terms of a specific origin, this is not particularly important to the present discussion, but I believe it can be pinpointed on a disciple of Confucius's named Fuzi 宓子, and I will have occasion to turn to it in chapter 3.

To give two examples of the discussion of *cheng* that may shed light on "All Things Flow into Form," consider, first, another text from the *Zhuangzi* called "Gengsang Chu" 庚桑楚. According to this discussion of someone who is able to *duxing* 獨行 ("walk alone"): 為不善乎顯明之中者, 人得而誅之; 為不善乎幽閒之中者, 鬼得而誅之; 明乎人、明乎鬼者, 然後能獨行 "He who does what is not good in clear and open view will be seized and punished by men. He who does what is not good in shadowed seclusion will be seized and punished by ghosts. Only he who is visible to both men and ghosts will then be able to walk alone."[9] Here the contrast between "clear and open view" (*xianming* 顯明) and "shadowed seclusion" (*youxian* 幽閒) indicates a play with light and darkness that also underlies the discussion of *ren bai wei cha* ("revealing oneself for inspection by others") in "All Things Flow into Form." As in *The Songs of the South*, *duxing* for "Gengsang Chu" refers to not only a person's walking alone but also the act of self-scrutiny as I turn my attention to myself. In so doing, I find nothing to hide and am "at ease with myself," or *zi ruo*, to recall the expression from "All Things Flow into Form." This corresponds to earlier in "Gengsang Chu." On the one hand, a person "prepares the bounty of things and goes along with external forms" (*bei wu yi jiang xing* 備物以將形). On the other, one is able to preserve a genuineness unaffected by what takes place on the outside: 藏

不虞以生心, 敬中以達彼 ("withdraw into thoughtlessness and in this way give life to your mind, and be reverent of what is within and extend this same reverence to others").[10] In "Gengsang Chu," this is defined later simply as *cheng ji* 誠己 ("being sincere to oneself").

"Gengsang Chu" continues with the statement: 券內者, 行乎無名 "He who acts according to what is on the inside does deeds that bring no fame." And this is followed by the elaboration: 行乎無名者, 唯庸有光 "For him who does deeds that bring no fame, his mediocrity shines forth a light." That is, he who looks inward as opposed to outward, even as he receives no recognition and appears wholly unimpressive, exhibits a light that is brighter than anyone else's. Here the word *quan* 券 is literally a tally that can be broken in two or more pieces; its being pieced back together will restore the integrity of the original. For one to *quan nei* 券內 ("act according to what is on the inside"), he is placing the same emphasis on the internal as "All Things Flow into Form" does with its formulation about the mind. As for the reference to a light, this refers back to the opening statement of "Gengsang Chu": 宇泰定者, 發乎天光; 發乎天光者, 人見其人, 物見其物[11] "He whose inner being rests in the great serenity will send forth a heavenly light. To send forth a heavenly light means that people will be seen for what they are and things will be seen for what they are." Once again, this discussion can be understood as providing a more elaborate explanation for the meaning of *ren bai wei cha* ("revealing oneself for inspection by others") in "All Things Flow into Form."[12]

The second example to be considered is from "Great Learning" (Daxue), the synoptic account of Confucian teaching that later became recognized as one of the "Four Books," in the discussion of what it means to *cheng qi yi* 誠其意 ("be sincere with one's intentions").[13] As with "Gengsang Chu," "The Great and Venerable Teacher," and poems from *The Songs of the South*, this discussion places some emphasis on the situation where a person is alone, as can be seen in the injunction: 故君子必慎其獨也 "Therefore the superior man will always be watchful over himself when alone." In one of its most memorable statements, "Great Learning" describes how the petty man acts futilely to hide his wrongdoings from others: 人之視己, 如見其肺肝, 然則何益矣 "But what is the use? For other people see him as if they see his lungs and liver." In the form of a rhetorical question, this underscores the same concern with transparency that we saw with "All Things Flow into Form."[14] In fact, just as "All Things Flow into Form" speaks of "the heart of hearts," "Great Learning" also draws attention to the mind: 富潤屋, 德潤身, 心廣體胖 "Wealth makes a house shining and virtue makes a person shining. When one's mind is broad and his heart generous, his body becomes big and is at ease." Presumably, it is only after the mind has prevailed and seized control of itself that it is able to expand, "becoming big and being at ease."[15] Finally, all of this discussion from "Great Learning" is centered on the notion of *cheng* 誠 ("sincerity"): 所謂誠其意者，毋自欺也，如惡惡臭，如好好色，此之謂自謙 "What is meant by making the will sincere is allowing no self-deception, as when we hate a bad smell or love a beautiful color. This is called satisfying oneself." One who does not *zi qi* 自欺 ("cheat himself") is one who is *zi qie* 自謙 ("satisfied with himself"), following the interpretation of the ancient commentator Zheng Xuan 鄭玄 (127–200). In the parlance of "All Things Flow into Form," this is *zi ruo* ("being at ease with himself").[16] If "Great Learning" is any indication, then being sincere is not so much following one's intuition as working hard to reach a state where one is able to naturally choose between what one likes and dislikes.[17]

If the analysis above is correct in suggesting that there is an ethical concern underlying "All Things Flow into Form," then at this point, we might step away from this text and take a broader view of the intellectual context that it was a part of. Suppose, for instance, that "All Things Flow into Form" was not written in a vacuum, that it was actually a reaction against another line of thinking, a realist position that stressed not the ruler's inner moral quality, but brute power; not one's own transparency and accountability, but the dominance and control of others. In contrast with the notion of *ren bai wei cha* ("revealing oneself for inspection by others"), we may recall the remark by a modern-day political scientist commenting on what he calls the "power paradox" in contemporary politics: "Power remains strong when it remains in the dark; exposed to the sunlight it begins to evaporate."[18] In the intellectual context of the Warring States, this position was most clearly expressed by Han Feizi 韓非子 (ca. 280–233 BCE).

Consider the following discussion from "Wielding the Scepter" (Yang quan 揚權):

用一之道，以名為首，名正物定，名倚物徙。故聖人執一以靜，使名自命，令事自定。不見其采，下故素正。

The way to put Oneness into use starts with names. When names are rectified, things will be settled; when names are slanted, things will shift around. Therefore, the sage holds Oneness in hand and rests in tranquility, letting names themselves make the appointments and affairs settle on their own. If his true colors are not shown, those below will be plain and upright."[19]

In both form and content, such a discussion tallies so closely to the *Laozi* 老子 that we might have mistaken one for the other but for the fact that Han Feizi elaborates on the same position elsewhere in his writings. This is "The Way of the Sovereign" (Zhudao 主道):

道者, 萬物之始, 是非之紀也。是以明君守始以知萬物之源, 治紀以知善敗之端。故虛靜以待[20], 令名自命也, 令事自定也。虛則知實之情, 靜則知動者正。有言者自為名, 有事者自為形。形名參同, 君乃無事焉, 歸之其情。故曰: 君無見其所欲; 君見其所欲, 臣自將雕琢。君無見其意; 君見其意, 臣將自表異。故曰: 去好去惡, 臣乃見素; 去智去舊[21], 臣乃自備。

Tao is the beginning of the myriad things, the standard of right and wrong. Thus the intelligent ruler, by holding to the beginning, knows the source of everything, and, by keeping to the standard, knows the origin of good and bad. Therefore, by resting empty and reposed, he waits and allows names themselves to make appointments and affairs to settle on their own. Empty, he knows the reality of fullness; reposed, he knows the correctness of action. Who utters a word creates himself a name; who has an affair creates himself a form. If the forms and names are compared and made to be identical, then the ruler will find nothing to worry about as everything returns to reality. Hence, "The ruler must not reveal his wants. For, if he reveals his wants, his ministers will polish their manners accordingly. The ruler must not reveal his views. For, if he reveals his views, the ministers will display their differences." Hence, "If the like and dislikes of the ruler be concealed, the plainness of the ministers will be revealed. If the wisdom and experience of the ruler be discarded, the ministers will take precautions."[22]

Comparing the two passages from Han Feizi, the close connection between them is unmistakable. In offering the following description of the ruler: 故虛靜以待, 令名自命也, 令事自定也 "By resting empty and reposed, he waits and allows names themselves to make appointments and affairs to settle on their own," "The Way of the Sovereign" matches "Wielding the Scepter" almost word for word: 故聖人執一以靜, 使名自命, 令事自定 "Therefore, the sage holds Oneness in hand and rests in tranquility, letting names themselves make the appointments and affairs settle on their own." And, at the end of "The Way of the Sovereign": 去好去惡, 臣乃見素; 去智去舊, 臣乃自備 "If the like and dislikes of the ruler be concealed, the plainness of the ministers will be revealed. If the wisdom and experience of the ruler be discarded, the ministers will take precautions." This can be seen as fuller expression of "Wielding the Scepter": 不見其采, 下故素正 "If his true colors are not shown, those below will be plain and upright." Such discussion makes it clear that the so-called true colors (*cai* 采) of the ruler are his preferences, or "likes and dislikes." Reveal them, and those below will vie for the ruler's favor and become opportunistic, competitive, and unfocused in their work. Conceal them, and the ministers are restored to their *su* 素 ("plainness"), a word that describes for Han Feizi not so much a state of mind but a situation of clear and direct command where the duties of the officials ("affairs") are matched with their titles ("names"). It is in this way that the ruler grasps the principle of Oneness or the Way, retreating into the background while maintaining oversight over all his subjects.

This relation between the ruler and his ministers is summed up in another text from Han Feizi, "The Two Handles" (Erbing 二柄), using the same catch phrase:

故曰:「去好去惡, 群臣見素。」群臣見素, 則大君不蔽矣。

If the like and dislikes of the ruler be concealed, the plainness of the ministers will be revealed. If the plainness of the ministers be revealed, the ruler never will be deluded.[23]

Such discussion indicates that everything starts at the top. A ruler who is deluded will not be able to staff the right personnel or evaluate them properly. That would be the beginning of chaos, and the consequences are too obvious to be spelled out.[24]

In all of these passages from Han Feizi, the main point is that the attribute of "plainness" (*su*) pertains not to the ruler but to those that he oversees and controls, with the real benefit that they would be kept in line. In contrast to this, the ruler himself remains dark and invisible, both everywhere and nowhere. Anything less would be disruptive to the efficient working of the state, and there is no mistaking the hierarchy between the ruler and the minister. The same hierarchy is reinforced in one more passage from Han Feizi, "On Assumers" (Shuo yi 說疑). After listing some fifteen famous ministers from the past, Han Feizi offers this characterization:

皆夙興夜寐，卑身賤體，竦心白意，明刑辟、治官職以事其君，進善言、通道法而不敢矜其善，有成功、立事而不敢伐其勞。

> They got up early in the morning and went to bed late at night, humbled themselves and debased their bodies; they were cautious in mind and plain in intention, and clarified penal action and attended to official duties in serving their rulers. When they presented good counsels to the throne and convinced their masters thoroughly of right laws, they dared not boast of their own goodness. When they achieved merits and accomplished tasks, they dared not show off their services.[25]

Here the expression *song xin bai yi* 竦心白意 ("cautious in mind and plain in intention") echoes *su* ("plainness") or *jian su* ("revealing one's plainness") from the previously examined passages. The subject is to serve the ruler wholeheartedly, absent of any personal preference or self-interest. In the same way, when the fifteen ministers are described as self-deprecating—that is, "not daring to boast of their own goodness" (*bugan fa qi lao* 不敢伐其勞)—this can be seen as consistent with the various discussions cited here, where the ministers adhere to their duties and are careful not to step beyond their allotted positions.

For my purposes, the contrast cannot be greater between the Han Feizi passages and the texts considered in the first part of this chapter, particularly "All Things Flow into Form." Both describe the transparency of a person, "All Things Flow into Form" with the phrase, *ren bai wei cha* ("revealing oneself for inspection by others"), and Han Feizi with *song xin bai yi* ("cautious in mind and plain in intention"). But whereas "All Things Flow into Form" is concerned with the mind and the possibility of its attaining a kind of purity that enables the mind to open itself to others, such inner dimension is nowhere to be found in Han Feizi. In fact, this talented thinker of the third century BCE seems to regard any kind of inclination arising from within as nothing more than "likes and dislikes," and even these are relevant only insofar as they concern the ruler, who must be careful to conceal them. This leads us to a second, more obvious point. In all of the Han Feizi passages, there is never any question to whom words like *bai* or *su* refer. It is the minister who bares his mind as a show of loyalty to the ruler, sticking to the responsibilities demanded by his post. While we do not know whether Han Feizi had any knowledge of "All Things Flow into Form," it is likely that it would not have mattered, just as he did not care for the theorizations about the mind, as observed just now. Han Feizi presented a picture of the political reality as he saw fit, and he had good reasons to think that this was always how things were.

As for "All Things Flow into Form," the discussion there does not directly identify who it is that should "reveal himself for inspection by others," but it is due to this reason that we might conclude that it is for everyone—that is, anyone who is in possession of a mind and can attempt to look for a mind within a mind. Though it is possible that these discussions are speaking past one another, using terms that are simply part of a common discourse, there is much to gain by putting them side by side and suggesting that "All Things Flow into Form" came onto the scene as a result of such discussions as those by Han Feizi. That is, this newly discovered text was an effort to push back on the demands a ruler placed on his subjects, pointing out, in effect, that the ruler must adhere to the same ethical standard. As we will see in the following chapter, it is precisely in the context of an argument (between a Confucian-minded adviser and a figure from the legalist tradition as prominent as Han Feizi) that we will find an exchange parallel to the one suggested here. This is a debate concerning the notion of self-struggle and how a person could overcome more base urges and rise up to a higher, more ethical standard.

For one example of this discussion of self-struggle, consider the following text from the "Zichan" 子產, a newly discovered Warring States manuscript now at Tsinghua University in Beijing.[26] This text consists of a series of evaluative comments about the eponymous figure, the renowned statesman from Zheng 鄭 who died in 522 BCE. One of them reads as follows (slips 3–5):

子產所旨 (嗜) 欲不可晢 (知)，內 (納) 君子亡厶 (偏)，官政眾帀 (師) 栗，堂 (當) 事乃進，亡好，曰固身菫＝諆＝ (謹信; 謹信) 又 (有) 事，所㠯 (以) 自尭 (勝) 立由 (中)，此胃 (謂) 亡好惡.

What Zichan desires cannot be known. In bringing in gentlemen he shows no special preference. In overseeing the various officials of the government, he is respectful, and he promotes them only to serve their duty, showing no favors. This is called integrity and trustworthiness. Because he serves with trustworthiness, he overcomes himself and sets the standard. This is called not having likes and dislikes.

In commenting on the leadership qualities of Zichan, this discussion is like the passages from Han Feizi, noting the correspondence between his personal desires (or the lack thereof) and the functioning of the government. The behavior of the leader has a direct impact on those below, and this is the reason that he must be cautious in his every word and action, not influencing the lower officials in any improper way, which might lead to some of the disastrous consequences that Han Feizi mentions. It is no surprise that Zichan is often described as a precursor of the legalist tradition to which Han Feizi belongs, an affiliation that has less to do with any direct connection than their common response to the demands necessitated by the realities of political power. Interestingly, the text uses *zi sheng li zhong* 自勝立中 ("to overcome oneself and set the standard") to describe Zichan's character. This is an intriguing phrase that not only resembles the formulation of "the heart of hearts" in "All Things Flow into Form" but also points to a set of ideas with a complex history of their own. Understanding these ideas will be crucial for a reading of "All Things Flow into Form." This is the subject of chapter 3.

CHAPTER 3

"The Heart of Hearts"

In considering the genealogy of the phrase *xin bu sheng xin* 心不勝心 ("if the mind does not prevail over the mind") from "All Things Flow into Form," we may begin with another manuscript from the Shanghai Museum, "The Gentlemen Enact the Rites" (Junzi wei li 君子為禮).[1] As has been noted by many scholars, this text bears an obvious resemblance to a passage in the *Analects* (Lunyu 論語), and one can raise interesting questions about this collection of Confucius's sayings based on the new source. For our purpose, "The Gentlemen Enact the Rites" is useful for uncovering ancient conceptions of the self-struggle that underlies "All Things Flow into Form."[2]

According to "The Gentlemen Enact the Rites" (slips 1–3):

䜖 (顏) 困 (淵) 㫑 (侍) 於夫＝子＝ (夫子。夫子) 曰:「韋 (回), 君子為豊 (禮), 吕 (以) 依於恳 (仁) 。」䜖 (顏) 困 (淵) 俀 (作) 而含 (答) 曰:「韋 (回) 不悔 (敏), 弗能少居也。」夫子曰:「迡 (坐), 虖 (吾) 語女 (汝) 。言之而不義, 口勿言也; 見 (視) 之而不義, 目勿見 (視) 也; 聖 (聽) 之而不義, 耳勿聖 (聽) 也; 達 (動) 而不義, 身毋達 (動) 安 (焉) 。」䜖 (顏) 困 (淵) 退, 䇿 (數) 日不出。〔□□問〕之曰:「虖 (吾) 子可 (何) 兀 (其) 膡 (瘠) 也?」曰:「朕 (然) 。虖 (吾) 新 (親) 睯 (聞) 言於夫子, 欲行之不能, 欲达 (去) 之而不可, 虖 (吾) 是以膡 (瘠) 也。」

Yan Yuan was serving the Master. The Master said, "Hui, the gentleman puts the rites into practice in order to accord with benevolence. Yan Yuan rose and responded, "Hui is not quick and is not able to settle firmly in it for a little while." The Master said, "Sit, let me tell you! If it is improper to speak, do not speak with your mouth. If it is improper to look, do not look with your eyes. If it is improper to listen, do not listen with your ears. If it is improper to move, do not move with your body." Yan Yuan withdrew and stayed in for several days. . . . Someone asked him, "Why is our master emaciated?" The reply: "That is so. I heard these teachings directly from the Master. Though I would like to put them into practice, I am unable to do so. Though I would like to cast them aside, I cannot permit it. This is why I am emaciated."

The close relation between this text and the *Analects* 12.1 is unmistakable:

顏淵問仁。子曰：「克己復禮為仁。一日克己復禮，天下歸仁焉。為仁由己，而由人乎哉？」顏淵曰：「請問其目。」子曰：「非禮勿視，非禮勿聽，非禮勿言，非禮勿動。」顏淵曰：「回雖不敏，請事斯語矣。」 [3]

Yan Yuan asked about benevolence. The Master said, "To return to the observance of the rites through overcoming the self constitutes benevolence. If for a single day a man could return to the observance of the rites through overcoming himself, then the whole Empire would consider benevolence to be his. However, the practice of benevolence depends on oneself alone, and not on others. Yan Yuan said, "I should like you to list the items." The Master said, "Do not look unless it is in accordance with the rites; do not listen unless it is in accordance with the rites; do not speak unless it is in accordance with the rites; do not move unless it is in accordance with the rites." Yan Yuan said, "Though Hui is not quick, I shall direct my efforts towards what you have said."

These two texts record the exchange between Confucius and Yan Yuan 顏淵 (who sometimes refers to himself by his personal name, Hui 回). In both cases, the discussion begins with Confucius's observation that "benevolence" (*ren* 仁) is the basis for the rites. In both cases, in response to the disciple's request for further clarification, the master elaborates by listing a series of prescriptions and by pointing out that whether it is looking, listening, speaking, or any movement at all, one must not deviate from the proper way. In both cases, Yan Yuan admits that this is beyond his grasp, and much work needs to be done before he is able to attain what Confucius has prescribed.

Similar as they are, the texts are, to be sure, not identical. Only "The Gentlemen Enact the Rites" refers to "propriety" (*yi* 義) or its lack thereof, but this is simply stating more explicitly a notion implied all along in the *Analects* 12.1. A more important difference is the adage *ke ji fu li* 克己復禮 ("Return to the observance of the rites through overcoming oneself"), found only in the *Analects*, and this parallels another comment by Confucius that appears at the end of a historical narrative in the *Zuo Tradition* (Zuozhuan 左傳), which can be considered in some detail.

In the twelfth year of Duke Zhao of Lu 魯昭公 (530 BCE), King Ling of Chu 楚靈王 was bent on expanding the power of his state. A wise adviser cautioned him of the risks by citing the example of an earlier ruler, who met with disaster because he "gave free rein to the desires of his heart" (*si qi xin* 肆其心). Upon hearing this, as reported by the narrative, the Chu ruler retreated into his room and reflected on the matter for several days (much like Yan Yuan in "The Gentlemen Enact the Rites"), but ultimately *buneng zike* 不能自克 ("was unable to overcome himself") and proceeded with his plans, meeting with the obvious results. The narrative ends with a comment by Confucius, here identified by his style:

仲尼曰：「古也有志：克己復禮，仁也。信善哉！楚靈王若能如是，豈其辱於乾谿？」⁴

> Zhongni said: "There is a maxim from times long past: 'To return to the observance of the rites through overcoming oneself—that is benevolence.' How true this is! If King Ling of Chu could have done this, how could he ever have been disgraced at Ganxi?"

As it is clear from Confucius's comment, the adage of "returning to the observance of the rites through overcoming oneself" did not originate with the venerated master; it must have been part of the received wisdom about which so little is known apart from the scant references in some surviving texts. While the source of the saying is nowhere indicated in the *Analects* 12.1, its repetition in Confucius's initial remark suggests that it is a statement in need of commentary, and this seems to confirm that it had been inherited by Confucius from a different source, which needs not be the *Zuo Tradition*. As for the relation between the *Analects* 12.1 and "The Gentlemen Enact the Rites," the adage also provides an important clue: the statement is so succinct and so powerful that it is difficult to imagine how it could have been overlooked if it had already been used in a discussion of benevolence and the rites. The fact that "The Gentlemen Enact the Rites" never mentions it hints at the early date of this newly discovered text. We might imagine that the *Analects* 12.1 came later, merging an ancient saying with sources related to "The Gentlemen Enact the Rites," if not that text itself.

These matters aside, it is interesting to read "The Gentlemen Enact the Rites" and the *Analects* 12.1 for what they say. Regardless of whether a discussion draws on the ancient saying, and regardless of which comes before which, these sources share the same conception of a self-struggle for overcoming one's desires. This conception is described in greater detail in "The Gentlemen Enact the Rites" and is the reason that this new discovery is so valuable. As seen in Yan Yuan's comment (made to a third party, whose identity is lost due to a lacunae in the text, but probably a student of his own), upon hearing the instruction from Confucius, Yan Yuan thinks hard about putting it into action but ultimately fails to do so.

For another instance of the same kind of self-struggle, involving not Yan Yuan but another disciple of Confucius's, Zixia 子夏, we can turn to a passage from Han Feizi's "Illustrations of Laozi's Teachings" (Yu Lao 喻老):

子夏見曾子。曾子曰:「何肥也?」對曰:「戰勝,故肥也。」曾子曰:「何謂也?」子夏曰:「吾入見先王之義則榮之,出見富貴之樂又榮之。兩者戰於胸中,未知勝負,故臞。今先王之義勝,故肥。」是以志之難也,不在勝人,在自勝也。故曰:「自勝之謂強。」[5]

Zixia saw Zengzi. Zengzi asked, "Why have you become so stout?" "Because I have been victorious in warfare," replied Zixia. "What do you mean by that?" asked Zengzi. In reply, Zixia said: "Whenever I went in and saw the propriety of the early kings I rejoiced in it. Whenever I went out and saw the pleasure of the rich and noble I rejoiced in it, too. These two conflicting attractions waged a war within my breast. When victory and defeat still hung in the balance, I was thin. Since the virtue of the early kings won the war, I have become stout." Therefore, the difficulty of volition lies not in conquering others but in conquering oneself. Hence the saying: "He who overcomes himself is strong."

As is customary with passages from "Illustrations of Laozi's Teachings," this discussion is centered around a quotation from the *Laozi*, in this case chapter 33: 自勝之謂強 "He who overcomes himself is strong."⁶ While the *Laozi* generally prefers "weakness" over "strength," here the discussion is not concerned with strength per se, only the strength for overcoming oneself. As explained in the commentary attributed to the legendary transmitter of the *Laozi*, Heshanggong 河上公, "overcoming oneself" means overcoming the unwanted, distracting desires that one might have; it is in this way, paradoxically, that one is able to dominate others: 人能自勝已情欲, 則天下無有能與己爭者, 故為強也 "If a man is able to vanquish the desires of his own character, then nobody in the world can fight him. Therefore he is strong."⁷ Understood this way, the quotation from the *Laozi* shares the same theme with Confucius's comment in the *Zuo Tradition*, "The Gentlemen Enact the Rites," and the *Analects* 12.1. As for Han Feizi's discussion surrounding the quotation from the *Laozi*, it is noteworthy that it refers to the "the propriety of the early kings" (*xianwang zhi yi* 先王之義): not only is "propriety" (*yi* 義) the same notion that we saw in "The Gentlemen Enact the Rites," but more importantly, the identification of the early kings suggests a kind of attribution similar to the citation of a maxim (*zhi* "record") in the *Zuo Tradition*. Both point to a common set of teachings transmitted from earlier times, or at least thought to be. To this group one could also add the "Zichan," mentioned at the end of chapter 2, which contains what is likely also a maxim: 自弆 (勝) 立申 (中) "To overcome oneself and establish a standard."

The most interesting aspect of Han Feizi's discussion in "Illustrations of Laozi's Teachings" is, of course, the reference to self-struggle and the ensuing changes in a person's physical mass. This is the same as what we find in "The Gentlemen Enact the Rites." Comparing the two, we might say that Zixia has successfully moved beyond the stage that Yan Yuan in "The Gentlemen Enact the Rites" is still stuck in. This is the reason that one is "emaciated" (*ji* 瘠) or "thin" (*qu* 臞), whereas the other is "stout" (*fei* 肥). It is also no accident that Zixia's interlocutor in "Illustrations of Laozi's Teachings" is Zengzi 曾子. Recall the statement attributed to him in "Great Learning": 富潤屋, 德潤身, 心廣體胖 "Wealth makes a house shining and virtue makes a person shining. When one's mind is broad and his heart generous, his body becomes big and is at ease."⁸ In the light of "Illustrations of Laozi's Teachings" and "The Gentlemen Enact the Rites," we might say that Zengzi's weight gain in "Great Learning" is due to his having made the right move to overcome his desires. Then, too, the "Great Learning" reference to a shining house echoes the struggle between "the propriety of the early kings" (*xianwang zhi yi*) and "the pleasure of the rich and noble" (*fugui zhi le* 富貴之樂), such as described in "Illustrations of Laozi's Teachings." An ideal person is able to resolve the conflict between the two, not by gaining actual material wealth but by embodying the ways of the ancient sages in such a way that the person is able to exhibit the qualities of possessing material wealth, as if somehow managing to achieve both at the same time.

Of course, from the perspective of "Illustrations of Laozi's Teachings," it is much more preferable if one could do away with these different obsessions and stop the pendulum swing from the teachings of the ancient sages to the pursuit of material wealth. This would be *zi sheng zhi wei qiang* ("he who overcomes himself is strong"): not falling victim to the desires arising from within that slowly eat one away. The same theme is retained in other versions of the same story, but the focus changes considerably. Consider the following passage from a text from the *Huainanzi* called "Quintessential Spirit" (Jingshen 精神). After citing the story of Zixia's self-struggle, the discussion continues with the following criticism against Confucian scholars in general:

推其志，非能不[9]貪富貴之位、不便侈靡之樂，直[10]迫性閉欲，以義自防也。雖情心鬱殪，形性屈竭，猶不得已自強也，故莫能終其天年。若夫至人，量腹而食，度形而衣，容身而游，適情而行，餘天下而不貪，委萬物而不利，處大廓之宇，游無極之野，登太皇，馮太一，玩天地於掌握之中，夫豈為貧富肥臞哉！故儒者非能使人弗欲，而能止之；非能使人勿樂，而能禁之。夫使天下畏刑而不敢盜，豈若能使無有盜心哉！[11]

Based on this, it is not that his will was able to not covet positions of wealth and honor and not appreciate the delights of excess; it was merely that by constraining his nature and restricting his desires that he used propriety to guard against them. Although their emotions and minds were depressed and gloomy and their bodies and natures were constricted and exhausted, they had no choice but to force themselves. Thus, none was able to live out his allotted years. Contrast these with the perfect men: they eat exactly what fills their bellies, they wear precisely what fits their forms. They roam by relaxing their bodies. They act by matching their genuine responses to the situation. If left the empire, they do not covet it. If entrusted with the myriad things, they do not profit from it. They rest in the vast universe, roam in the country of the limitless, ascend Grand August, and ride Grand One. They play with Heaven and earth in the palms of their hands: how is it possible that people like them would grow fat or thin by coveting wealth? Thus, because the Confucians are unable to prevent people from desiring, they can only try to stop them from being fulfilled. Because they are unable to prevent people from delighting in things, they can only try to forbid these delights. They cause the world to fear punishments and not dare to steal, but how can they cause people not to have the intention to steal?

A discussion such as this is by no means an endorsement of the pursuit of material wealth, but it also recognizes that such pursuit is all too natural, and Zixia and other Confucian scholars are wrong to try to suppress that urge. Here, the language used to describe this suppression reads like a direct commentary on the *Analects* 12.1 and "The Gentlemen Enact the Rites"; note, once again, the use of the word "propriety" (*yi*) in the phrase "using propriety to guard against [one's own desires]" (*yi yi zi fang* 以義自防). By contrast, the "perfect men" (*zhiren* 至人) are different. When "Quintessential Spirit" suggests that their bodies do not change whether they are rich or poor, this is clearly a reference to Zixia's situation, reported earlier in the same passage. In this way, this text from the *Huainanzi* echoes Han Feizi's "Illustrations of Laozi's Teachings." The point is not to adhere to the teachings of the ancient sages or to give up one's desires but to attain the freedom that results from transcending those endeavors.[12]

The theme of freedom is stated even more explicitly in a variation of the Yan Yuan/Zixia story, in an exchange between Zhongshan Gongzi Mou 中山公子牟 and Zhanzi 瞻子 that is attested in several ancient texts.[13] Here, the options of self-struggle are defined as material success and freedom. While the choice is obvious, should one fail to choose it for whatever reason (and herein lies the real lesson), one should simply accept the outcome and not force it any other way. That, according to this discussion, would only bring further harm to the person, what it calls "double injury" (*chongshang* 重傷).[14] Here is the story as told in the *Zhuangzi* text called "Giving Away a Throne" (Rang wang 讓王).

中山公子牟謂瞻子曰：「身在江海之上，心居魏闕之下，奈何？」瞻子曰：「重生。重生則輕利。」中山公子牟曰：「雖知之，未能自勝也。」瞻子曰：「不能自勝則從。」「神無惡乎？」「不能自勝而強不從者，此之謂重傷。重傷之人，无壽類矣。」魏牟，萬乘之公子也，其隱巖穴也，難為於布衣之士；雖未至乎道，可謂有其意矣。15

Prince Mou of Wei, who was living in Zhongshan, said to Zhanzi, "My body is here beside these rivers and seas, but my mind is still back there beside the palace towers of Wei. What should I do about it?" Zhanzi said, "Attach more importance to life! He who regards life as important will think lightly of material gain." Prince Mou said, "I know that's what I should do, but I can't overcome my inclinations." Zhanzi said, "If you can't overcome your inclinations, then follow them!" "But won't that do harm to the spirit?" "If you can't overcome your inclinations and yet you try to force yourself not to follow them, this is to do a double injury to yourself. Men who do such double injury to themselves are never found in the ranks of the long-lived." Wei Mou was a prince of a state of ten thousand chariots, and it was more difficult for him to retire and live among the cliffs and caves than for an ordinary person. Although he did not attain the Way, we may say that he had the will to do so.

Compared to the "perfect men" (*zhiren*) of "Quintessential Spirit," Prince Mou is someone who is still finding his way and not yet "arrived." This is the import of the final observation of the "Giving Away a Throne": 雖未至乎道，可謂有其意矣 "Although he did not attain the Way, we may say that he had the will to do so." This being said, the discussion is clear that it would be disastrous if he were to insist on such a pursuit. The notion of "double injury" (*chongshang*) highlights a concern with physical well-being that can be examined in greater detail.

For scholars like A. C. Graham, the concern with physical well-being as seen in the passage from "Giving Away a Throne" betrays an intellectual affiliation with the teachings of the obscure Warring States thinker Yang Zhu 楊朱 (fifth century BCE).16 The same concern can be found in a text from the *Annals of Lü Buwei* (Lüshi Chunqiu 呂氏春秋) called "Making Life the Foundation" (Ben sheng 本生), another Yangist text identified by Graham. Here the discussion begins by pointing out that a man's task is to cultivate what Nature, or "Heaven" (*Tian* 天), has endowed him with. A person who is able to do so is "the Son of Heaven" (*Tianzi* 天子), an epithet that would later be reserved exclusively for the ruler. As "Making Life the Foundation" goes on to refer to the officials under the command of this "Son of Heaven," it draws on a metaphor about the mind and senses shared by several ancient accounts: the ruler oversees the officials, just as the mind controls the senses and risks being overrun by them if one indulged in sensual desires without restraint.[17] This is followed by a further but not unrelated metaphor, that of war. According to "Making Life the Foundation," one who does not follow the natural course of things is waging a war against oneself. This is the passage in full:

> 始生之者，天也；養成之者，人也。能養天之所生而勿攖之，謂天子。天子之動也，以全天為故者也。此官之所自立也，立官者以全生也。今世之惑主，多官而反以害生，則失所為立之矣。譬之若修兵者，以備寇也。今修兵而反以自攻，則亦失所為修之矣。[18]

> Heaven is what first engenders life; Man is what fulfills that life by nurturing it. The person who is capable of nurturing the life that Heaven has created without doing violence to it is called the Son of Heaven. The purpose of all the Son of Heaven's activity is to keep intact what is natural. This is the origin of the offices of government. The purpose of establishing them was to keep life intact. The deluded lords of the present age have multiplied the offices of government and are using them to harm life—this is missing the purpose for establishing them. Consider the example of training soldiers: soldiers are trained to prepare against bandits; but if one trained soldiers to attack himself instead, then the original reason for the training has been lost.

For the purposes of this study, it is not difficult to see how the metaphor of war connects with all of the texts discussed in this chapter: if the indulgence of one's desires is like waging a war against oneself, then a person who has reined in these desires is one who has "overcome himself," the meaning of both *zi sheng* and *ke ji*. Note how the expression used by "Making Life the Foundation," or *zi gong* 自攻 ("to attack oneself") echoes with another statement later in the same text: 靡曼皓齒，鄭、衛之音，務以自樂，命之曰伐性之斧 "Languid limbs and gleaming teeth and the tunes of Zheng and Wei—people are devoted to these to bring themselves pleasure, but they should be called 'axes that hack at one's inborn nature,'" for which I would especially emphasize the word *fa* 伐 ("to hack").[19] This statement continues the metaphor of war, but it is even more specific: the desire for sensual pleasure is like the instruments used to reduce and diminish oneself, bit by bit. Needless to say, one should try to avoid this kind of self-harm. For "Making Life the Foundation," this means following the natural course of things and maintaining a balance that corresponds to the order of Heaven.[20]

In the light of these discussions, we may turn to Mencius again and revisit the passage about Ox Mountain from 6A8, introduced in chapter 1. Recall the statement: 其所以放其良心者，亦猶斧斤之於木也，旦旦而伐之，可以為美乎 "A man's letting go of his true heart is like the case of the trees and the axes. When the trees are lopped day after day, is it any wonder that they are no longer fine?"[21] Here we find Mencius denouncing the same kind of violence inflicted on oneself, and he stops short of calling it "the axes that hack at one's nature," as seen in "Making Life the Foundation." The more important difference, of course, is that Mencius understands this inner core needing protection from violence as also consisting of the roots of goodness, or what he calls "the true heart" (*liangxin* 良心). Note how Mencius cautions against "letting go" (*fang* 放) of it, a term that corresponds to "following along" (*cong* 從) in "Giving Away a Throne" of the *Zhuangzi*, as seen earlier: 不能自勝而強不從者，此之謂重傷 "If you can't overcome your inclinations and yet you try to force yourself not to follow them, this is to do a double injury to yourself."[22] Whereas Mencius is concerned with keeping the heart intact and protecting the goodness inherent in it, "Giving Away a Throne" focuses on setting it loose, particularly the desires that arise naturally from within and that we should simply go along with. The two discussions are coming from opposite directions, even though they share the same interest in the actions that can be directed at what is internal to oneself.

In the transmitted writings attributed to Mencius, we find several discussions that more clearly spell out the different inclinations internal to oneself, all near the Ox Mountain passage in 6A8. In 6A7, the mind is compared to the other senses: just as everyone is attracted to fine food, every mind is pleased by "reason" (*li* 理) and "rightness" (*yi* 義).[23] Clearly, Mencius's preference is for the mind, not the senses, and this is what sets him apart from "Making Life the Foundation" and the other Yangist passages cited earlier, for which the mind, if it is mentioned at all, is simply a part of what we are naturally endowed with. While we should look after it and make sure that it is not abused in any way, there is no reason to privilege it over the other parts of our natural makeup—that is, the senses. This cannot be more different from Mencius, whose view about the inherent goodness in all humans leads him to focus on the mind, the faculty with the capacity for "reason" and "rightness." Thus, in 6A15, he identifies the mind as the "greater body" (*dati* 大體) and the other senses as the "lesser bodies" (*xiaoti* 小體). In 6A14, he elaborates as follows: 體有貴賤, 有小大; 無以小害大, 無以賤害貴 "The parts of the person differ in value and importance. Never harm the parts of greater importance for the sake of those of smaller importance, or the more valuable for the sake of the less valuable."[24]

It is in this context that we return to "All Things Flow into Form" and the formulation of *xin bu sheng xin* 心不勝心 "If the mind does not prevail over the mind" that is the focus of the present chapter. This text describes the conflict between the different inclinations of oneself in terms of a battle, such that one constituent of the mind can *sheng* 勝 ("prevail over") another. We can see that this is directly descended from the notion of overcoming one's desires, reflected in various maxims such as "Return to the observance of the rites through overcoming oneself" (*ke ji fu li*) or "He who overcomes himself is strong" (*zi sheng zhi wei qiang*). We may also use this opportunity to refer to several related formulations.[25] These include *xin zhi zhong you you xin* 心之中又有心 ("a mind inside the mind"), seen in two closely related texts from the *Guanzi* 管子: "Inner Workings" (Neiye 內業) and "Art of the Mind, Part Two" (Xinshu xia 心術下).[26] And there is also a text from the *Records of the Rites* (Liji 禮記) called "Rites in the Formation of Character" (Liqi 禮器) as well as the newly excavated "Five Conducts" (Wuxing), both of which distinguish between an "outer mind" (*waixin* 外心) and an "inner mind" (*zhongxin* 中心 or *neixin* 內心).[27] While none of these related formulations uses the metaphor of war that is so central to "All Things Flow into Form," the contrast between one part of the mind and another, and thus the possibility of their being pitted against each other, is always present. The last of these examples is also useful for giving a more specific indication of when these formulations (which I call "the heart of hearts") might have emerged, because the distinction of an outer versus inner mind appears only in a commentary on the "Five Conducts" and not the text itself: it must have occurred at some point after the "Five Conducts" but before the commentary. This is consistent with the evidence from Mencius, cited earlier, since Mencius is traditionally said to be an intellectual descendant of the same Zisi 子思 with whom "Five Conducts" is so closely associated, and thus at some remove from that figure.[28]

For another example of "the heart of hearts" formulation, but one that postdates Mencius, we may turn to a text from the *Zhuangzi*, "The

Sign of Virtue Complete" (De chong fu 德充符). Here, in an exchange with Wang Tai 王駘, a man with "wordless teachings and some formless way of bringing the mind to completion" (*buyan zhi jiao, wuxing er xin cheng zhe* 不言之教、无形而心成者), an interlocutor poses the following question to none other than Confucius: 彼為己, 以其知得其心, 以其心得其常心, 物何為最之哉 "In the way he goes about it, he uses his knowledge to get at his mind, and uses his mind to get at the constant mind; why should things gather around him?" Notice the suggestion that it is by the means of "the mind" (*xin*) that one can come into possession of "the constant mind" (*changxin* 常心). The distinction between the two resembles "the heart of hearts" formulation and implies an indebtedness to that body of discourse. In his reply, Confucius makes a pun: 人莫鑑於流水而鑑於止水, 唯止能止眾止 "Men do not mirror themselves in running water—they mirror themselves in still water. Only what is still can still the stillness of other things." And, again, in referring to the example of Shun as someone who acts according to the ways of Nature: 受命於天, 唯舜獨也正, 幸能正生, 以正眾生 "Among those that receive the mandate from Heaven, only Shun sets the order. Luckily he was able to order his own life, and thereby order the lives of other things."²⁹ The repetitiousness in these responses hints at prolonged reflection on the question posed by the interlocutor, and it seems to me to represent Zhuangzi's own take, while borrowing the formulation of "the heart of hearts," on what constitutes the perfect sage.³⁰

If the discussion here is correct, that Mencius played a role in the discourse surrounding the formulation of "the heart of hearts," then Zhuangzi's borrowing of the same formulation suggests a development post-Mencius. This is a relation parallel to what some scholars have observed about Mencius 2A2 and another text from the *Zhuangzi*, "In the World of Men" (Renjianshi 人間世).³¹ In both cases, an "Inner chapter" from Zhuangzi, usually regarded as the core of his teachings, uses much of the same language seen in Mencius but turns the message completely upside down. What this means is that Zhuangzi was following closely in the footsteps of Mencius—a finer distinction than the traditional view that both figures lived during the fourth century BCE.³² Looking ahead, "The Sign of Virtue Complete" also anticipates Xunzi with such themes seen in Confucius's reply as quiescence and the concentration of one's mind as a means for unifying the world. Ironically, it is in Xunzi that we find a criticism of "the heart of hearts" formulation, which separates him from all the other texts discussed here.

"The Heart of Hearts" | 55

A second example of "the heart of hearts" formulation that I will discuss is from a text from the *Annals of Lü Buwei* called "On Necessary Conditions and Preparations" (Jubei 具備).³³ Here we find the statement: 故誠有誠乃合於情，精有精乃通於天 "Therefore, when sincerity is made more sincere, one is conjoined with the true nature of things. Only when the vital essences are made more essential does one commune with Heaven." By suggesting that one can bypass what is usually taken to be "sincerity" (*cheng*) and somehow grasp a better and more improved version of it, this seems to me to resemble the conception of "the heart of hearts." The same is also true with "essence" (*jing* 精), though it is a discussion of "sincerity" that I believe can lead us to an insight about the very origin of this important notion.

The statement cited here comes from the mouth of an anonymous commentator; it appears at the end of a narrative about Fuzi 宓子, a disciple of Confucius, and his governing of a small city called Shanfu 亶父.³⁴ According to this narrative, Fuzi had instructed the people of Shanfu not to poach young fish, and they were careful to follow this instruction even when fishing at night, with no one looking.³⁵ This so impressed Wuma Qi 巫馬期, another disciple of Confucius and a figure often seen together with Fuzi, that he went to Confucius and reported what he saw to the master:

宓子之德至矣。使民闇行，若有嚴刑於旁。敢問宓子何以至於此?

Master Fu's virtue is perfect! He causes people to act in the dark as if there were a strict punishment at hand. May I ask how Master Fu has achieved these results?

To which Confucius replies:

丘嘗與之言曰：『誠乎此者刑乎彼』。宓子必行此術於亶父也。

I, Qiu, once said to him: "Sincerity in oneself serves as a model for others." Master Fu must be practicing this method in Shanfu.

This exchange is significant for two reasons. One is the reference to "acting in the dark" (*anxing* 闇行) by Wuma Qi, and it is not difficult to see how this is related to the discussion of sincerity: sincerity is what sustains a person even in those moments when no one is looking, and the effort to attain it (and not just any form of sincerity but one that is more sincere than what is commonly known as sincerity) only highlights the importance of this notion. This anticipates my discussion in the following chapter, where I take on other expressions related to "acting in the dark." Equally crucial is Confucius's remark, which claims that the teaching of sincerity originated with him. We may compare this with a parallel passage in the *Huainanzi* called "Responses of the Way" (Daoying 道應), where Confucius asks Fuzi to explain the principle of his governing, and the disciple, not the master, replies: 誠於此者刑於彼 "Sincerity in oneself serves as a model for others."[36] Regardless of who said it first, what is important is that Fuzi plays the most critical role in the transmission of this teaching, with Confucius's validation. I would venture to say that this is where we should locate the origin of *cheng* ("sincerity"). A more precise way of stating this is that early advocates of *cheng* used this or other closely related texts to claim the origin of this notion. Such a discussion would not have been necessary—indeed possible—if *cheng* was already well established and widely circulating.

Throughout this chapter, we have considered "Return to the observance of the rites through overcoming oneself" (*ke ji fu li*), "He who overcomes himself is strong" (*zi sheng zhi wei qiang*), and other related statements that describe the same kind of self-struggle as "if the mind does not prevail over the mind" (*xin bu sheng xin*) from "All Things Flow into Form." While all of these discussions share the same basic theme, there is much variation in terms of the particular topic that a text focuses on, ranging from the constraining of one's desires to freedom, personal well-being, and cultivating the fundamental goodness inherent in oneself. There is one more variation of this that deserves mentioning: the understanding of *zi sheng* as a show of power, not "overcoming oneself" as seen in some of the texts already discussed, but "becoming victorious oneself." For this we can turn to the writings attributed to Shang Yang 商鞅, the prominent Qin statesman of the fourth century BCE. In a passage from the *Book of Lord Shang* (Shangjunshu 商君書) called "Charting the Policies" (Hua ce 畫策), we find the following discussion about how a ruler can be "clear-sighted" (*ming* 明) and "strong" (*qiang* 彊):

所謂明者，無所不見，則群臣不敢為姦，百姓不敢為非。是以人主處匡床之上，聽絲竹之聲，而天下治。所謂明者，使眾不得不為。所謂彊者，天下勝。天下勝，是故合力。是以勇彊不敢為暴，聖知不敢為詐而虛用。兼天下之眾，莫敢不為其所好，而辟其所惡。所謂彊者，使勇力不得不為己用。其志足，天下益之；不足，天下說

之。恃天下者,天下去之; 自恃者, 得天下。得天下者, 先自得者也。能勝彊敵者, 先自勝者也。³⁷

He who is clear-sighted sees everything, so that the ministers dare not behave villainously and the hundred clans dare not transgress. Hence, the ruler rests on a comfortable bed and listens to the sounds of music instruments made of silk and bamboo, and the world is well-ordered. What is called clear-sighted means making it so that the multitudes have no choice but to act on his behalf. He who is strong overpowers the world. With the world overpowered, strength is combined. Thus the courageous and strong dare not act violently; the sage and the knowledgeable dare not cheat and serve without making real input. With the multitudes of the world united, none dares not do what the ruler likes and avoid what he detests. He who is strong makes it so the courageous and powerful have no choice but to serve him. If his desires are satisfied, the world will satisfy him even more; if not, the world will attempt to please him. He who relies on the world, the world will abandon him. He who relies on himself will gain possession of the world. He who gains possession of the world is one who first gains possession of himself. He who is able to overpower a strong enemy is one who is able to first become victorious himself.

As with all the other texts considered in this chapter, this discussion touches on the question of what to do with one's desires. But rather than overcoming them, "Charting the Policies" emphasizes the upholding of such desires as a kind of absolute standard so they can be imposed on the people. This is seen in the statement: 兼天下之眾, 莫敢不為其所好, 而辟其所惡 "With the multitudes of the world united, none dares not do what the ruler likes and avoid what he detests."³⁸ Here we go back to the conception of desire as one's likes and dislikes, as seen in the Yangist texts considered above. "Charting the Policies" goes on to point out that the strength of the ruler depends on the strength of his people, all of which must be mustered for his own use: 所謂彊者, 使勇力不得不為己用 "He who is strong makes it so the courageous and powerful have no choice but to serve him." Thus, the ideal ruler for "Charting the Policies" is someone who maintains a tight grip on his people, holding all private desires in check so as to keep special interests from coming into their own. There is no room for the cultivation of any kind of inner dimension, no reference to the steps that one might take to strengthen oneself. Instead, for "Charting the Policies," *zi sheng* is very much the imposition of one's dominance over someone else. The aggression is directed outward, not inward.

For another attestation of the expression *zi sheng* seen in connection with Shang Yang, we may turn to the biography of the man himself as recorded in the *Grand Scribe's Records* (Shiji 史記). Here we find Shang Yang in the presence of Zhao Liang 趙良, a visitor who makes no attempt to conceal his intellectual allegiance as he opens his remark to Shang Yang with a quotation from Confucius. Zhao continues with the following comment:

> 反聽之謂聰，內視之謂明，自勝之謂彊。虞舜有言曰：『自卑也尚矣。』君不若道虞舜之道，無為問僕矣。[39]

> To turn listening inward is what is meant by keen-eared; to gaze within is what is meant by sharp-eyed; to overcome oneself is what is meant by strong. As Shun of Yu said, "One who lowers himself is elevated." It would be better for your lordship to follow the way of Shun of Yu; do not inquire from your servant.

As in the discussion from the *Book of Lord Shang*, here Zhao's comment dwells on the perceptiveness of the ruler, though the purpose of this is completely different: rather than looking to his subjects and dominating them, the ruler pays attention to himself, as indicated by the expressions *fanting* 反聽 ("turning listening inward") and *neishi* 內視 ("gazing within"). With the formulation *zi sheng zhi wei qiang* ("He who overcomes himself is strong"), Zhao Liang goes back to the adage exactly as it is stated in the *Laozi*, and indeed, understands it much in the same way, to overcome one's own desires. This is confirmed by matching the saying with a maxim attributed to the sage ruler Shun: 自卑也尚矣 "One who lowers himself is elevated." The self-effacement of this last saying suggests once again action directed at oneself as opposed to others.

In the context of Shang Yang's biography, the advice from Zhao Liang ultimately goes unheeded by our subject, and the powerful statesman, as is well-known, ends up dying a violent death (and here the moral overtone resembles the *Zuo Tradition* narrative cited at the beginning of this chapter). But this is really beside the point. What is most significant about the biography is the setup of a debate between two positions: one calls for the man in power to overcome his desires, much in the same way as the

Analects 12.1, *Zuo Tradition*, and the *Laozi*; the other makes the opposite point, that the powerful should impose his desires on his people as a show of his dominance. Because Shang Yang and the work attributed to him are generally later than those other sources, one might be inclined to see his position as a kind of response to, perhaps even backlash against, the call for self-cultivation. But another possibility—which seems more likely to me—is that the position represented by Shang Yang was always there. If the remark by Zhao Liang is any indication, the urging for the ruler to inspect himself was the outcome, not the cause. It was an attempt to address the abuse of power that must have been a concern for statesmen and thinking individuals as far back as we would allow.[40]

At this point, we might go back to "The Gentlemen Enact the Rites," where one finds a second passage following the one cited at the beginning of this chapter, cautioning a person to guard against being *duzhi* 蜀 (獨) 智 (知), *dugui* 蜀 (獨) 貴, and *dufu* 蜀 (獨) 賻 (富), such that they are *ren suo wu ye* 人所亞 (惡) 也 ("what people detest"). The rest of the passage, though partly damaged, contains Confucius's instruction on how the ruler should draw on the support of his people to improve himself, perhaps in the three areas of *zhi* 知 ("knowing"), *gui* 貴 ("being eminent"), and *fu* 富 ("being wealthy") mentioned just now. While this passage (slips 3, 9a+4, 9bd) appears to be self-contained and can be read entirely on its own, it is tempting to look for a connection with the earlier passage in light of what I have just suggested. On the one hand, there is the urging that one should overcome his desires (first passage). On the other hand, one is cautioned against being too arrogant, stubborn, and selfish (second passage). The two represent two positions in a single debate in the same way that Zhao Liang and Shang Yang come head to head in the *Grand Scribe's Records*. Once again, there is little doubt where "The Gentlemen Enact the Rites" stands, but I would suggest that it was precisely due to positions such as Shang Yang's that "The Gentlemen Enact the Rites" came to be written in this way.[41] Understood as such, the word *du* in "The Gentlemen Enact the Rites" takes on an added layer of meaning. As arrogance, stubbornness, selfishness, and absolute power, it is what one wants to overcome through self-scrutiny and introspection, the kind of meditative process that is often denoted by the expression *shen qi du* 慎其獨 ("to be watchful over oneself when alone"). Without this injunction, there is nothing to hold the ruler's power in check. Without the ruler's ever-growing appetite for power, we may not understand why there exists a need for "I the lone man" to take a pause and look deeply within. Such is the interwoven relation between these two positions. It goes without saying that only one of the two positions pays any attention to the mind.

It remains for me to discuss the essay from Xunzi called "An Exhortation to Learning" (Quanxue 勸學). According to the concluding passage of this text:

君子知夫不全不粹之不足以為美也, 故誦數以貫之, 思索以通之, 為其人以處之, 除其害者以持養之。使目非是無欲見也, 使耳非是無欲聞也, 使口非是無欲言也, 使心非是無欲慮也。及至其致好之也, 目好之五色, 耳好之五聲, 口好之五味, 心利之有天下。是故權利不能傾也, 群眾不能移也, 天下不能蕩也。生乎由是, 死乎由是, 夫是之謂德操。德操然後能定, 能定然後能應。能定能應, 夫是之謂成人。天見其明, 地見其光, 君子貴其全也。

The gentleman, knowing well that being incomplete and impure does not deserve to be called fine, recites that he will be familiar with them, ponders over that he will fully penetrate their meaning, acts in his person that he will put them into practice, and eliminates what is harmful that he will hold on to and nourish them. Thereby he causes his eye to be unwilling to see what is not correct, his ears unwilling to hear what is not correct, his mouth unwilling to speak anything not correct, and his mind unwilling to contemplate anything not correct. When he has reached the limit of such perfection, he finds delight in it. His eye then finds greater enjoyment in the five colors, his ear in the five sounds, his mouth in the five tastes, and his mind benefits from possessing all that is in the world. Therefore, the exigencies of time and place and considerations of personal profit cannot influence him, cliques and coteries cannot sway him, and the whole world cannot move him. He was born to follow it, and he will die following it: truly this can be called "being resolute from virtue." Keep resolute from virtue because only then can you be firm of purpose. Be firm of purpose because only then can you be responsive to all. One who can be both firm of purpose and responsive to all is truly to be called "the perfected man." Heaven shows its brilliance, Earth its vast expanses, and the gentleman values his completeness.[42]

While there is no mention of overcoming one's desires, this discussion does speak of the mind as well as the other senses acting according to what is correct, and in this way the passage resembles both "The Gentlemen Enact the Rites" and the *Analects* 12.1.⁴³ More interesting is how the discussion goes on to describe the ideal person: having thus perfected himself, he is so determined that he becomes somehow insulated from the influences of the world: 是故權利不能傾也, 群眾不能移也, 天下不能蕩也 "Therefore, the exigencies of time and place and considerations of personal profit cannot influence him, cliques and coteries cannot sway him, and the whole world cannot move him." This description resembles the absolute ruler in the *Book of Lord Shang*. Of course, here Xunzi is describing a man who is "being resolute from virtue" (*de cao* 德操), not a dictator, and his concern with learning and what is internal to oneself set him apart from the legalist tradition with which Han Feizi and Shang Yang are associated. Still, in the context of the discussion in this chapter, this passage from Xunzi raises a question: while adhering to the ideal of being uncompromising and single-minded, how far does one go before going too far? In chapter 4, I will have occasion to examine further the thought of this unique thinker who stood at the intersection between the different intellectual currents of the third century BCE.

CHAPTER 4

Walking in the Night

As mentioned in my discussion of "The Great and Venerable Teacher" of the *Zhuangzi* and "All Things Flow into Form," implicit in the expression *zhao che* ("arriving by dawn") is the notion of a journey in the night, a moment of self-scrutiny when a person is faced with no one but oneself, the beginning of a process of self-cultivation. This is a notion that I would like to examine in some detail in this chapter. I start by considering several expressions that describe this kind of nocturnal activity in the transmitted literary record, including *yexing* 夜行 and *xiaoxing* 宵行, both "walking by night"; *yinxing* 隱行 and *yinxing* 陰行, both "acting in secret"; and *qianxing* 潛行 "acting under cover."[1] I then turn to a fable about a man frightened by his own shadow, recorded in Xunzi's essay "Dispelling Blindness" (Jie bi 解蔽). I will show that this fable contains Xunzi's criticism against a rival thinker, someone who might have known a thing or two about the teachings reflected in "All Things Flow into Form." Understanding the nature of Xunzi's disagreement with this figure will allow us to better appreciate "All Things Flow into Form" and the controversy that it might have generated.

    In many ancient accounts, the notion of a journey in the night is associated with the ruler's capacity to attract his subjects regardless of their distance. Just how this is done is never clearly spelled out, and perhaps this is the point, given that great power is always unconventional, unpredictable, even somewhat mysterious. Thus, in a text from the *Huainanzi* called "Surveying Obscurities" (Lan ming 覽冥), we find the statement: 故召遠者, 使無為焉; 親近者, 言無事焉; 惟夜行者為能有之 "Thus to summon those who are far-off, emissaries are of no use; to cherish those who are close by, words are of no avail. Only one who walks by night is able to have this."[2]

In another text from the same collection, "Profound Precepts" (Miucheng 繆稱), the reference to "walking by night" is preceded by the statement: 動於近，成文於遠 "Actions undertaken near at hand cause a civilizing influence to spread far away."[3] Finally, in a text from the *Guanzi* called "Conditions and Circumstances" (Xingshi 形勢), there is a passage that is almost identical with "Surveying Obscurities" from the *Huainanzi*: 召遠者，使無為焉；親近者，言無事焉；唯夜行者獨有之[4]也 "For summoning those who are far-off, emissaries are of no use. For cherishing those who are close by, words are of no avail. Only one who walks by night has the capacity for such things."[5] Interestingly, in the commentary that accompanies this last text, "Explanations for 'Conditions and Circumstances'" (Xingshi jie 形勢解), there appears a definition of *yexing* as *xinxing* 心行 ("movement of the mind"). According to this commentary:

明主之使遠者來而近者親也，為之在心。所謂夜行者，心行也。能心行德，則天下莫能與之爭矣。故曰：「唯夜行者獨有之乎！」[6]

The enlightened ruler's capacity for making those far away come to him and those near at hand have close relationships with him depends on his heart. What is called "walking by night" refers to the movement of the mind. If the ruler is able to exercise virtue with his mind, no one in the world will be able to contend with him. Thus, it is said, "Only one who walks by night has the capacity for such things."

For this commentary to assert that *yexing* is *xinxing*, it is drawing attention to the internal, mental aspects of the notion. This is not exactly unexpected, since *xinxing* already appears in another passage in "Conditions and Circumstances" and is there described in terms that resemble *yexing*: 四方所歸，心行者也 "The four directions will turn to he who acts from his mind."[7] In this way, the commentary collapses two expressions that have a close bearing on one another. As we will see in "All Things Flow into Form," the attempt to link these two notions is not exclusive to this commentary from the *Guanzi*.

For a more concrete illustration of the ruler's attraction on his subjects, we may turn to an account about King Wen 文王, one of the founders of the Western Zhou, recorded in the *Grand Scribe's Records*, under "Basic Annals of Zhou" (Zhou benji 周本紀). This account opens with the statement: 西伯陰行善，諸侯皆來決平 "The Lord of the West carried out good deeds in secret, and the feudal lords all came to him to have their cases weighed."⁸ With the expression *yinxing* ("acting in secret"), the account emphasizes that King Wen's acts of kindness were not motivated by the want of fame or popuarlity. Yet, paradoxically, it was this lack of self-interest that drew the feudal lords to him. The account goes on to describe how the rulers of Yu 虞 and Rui 芮 arrived in Zhou only to witness the civility of the people there and feel ashamed about their own litigiousness. Thus, by virtue of his accomplishments at home, King Wen was able to exert an influence abroad, a perfect illustration of the attraction of the ruler described in the *Huainanzi* and *Guanzi*. Interestingly, in another version of this story, found in a text from the *Garden of Sayings* (Shuoyuan 說苑) called "The Lord's Way" (Jundao 君道), the account is followed by a comment by Confucius: 大哉！文王之道乎，其不可加矣！不動而變，無為而成，敬慎恭己而虞、芮自平 "So great is the way of King Wen that nothing more can be added to it! Without moving, he caused change; without acting, he accomplished success. By his being cautious and reverential, Yu and Rui were able to settle their dispute."⁹ Here the descriptions of "not moving" (*budong* 不動) and "not acting" (*wu wei* 無為) echo the discussions of *yexing* cited earlier, particularly the suggestion that the attractive ruler employs no emissaries and uses no words.¹⁰ King Wen "did not act" in the sense that he did not purposely try to attract the rulers of Yu and Rui. Instead, by quietly going about and acting in the best interests of others, he was able to transform the state of Zhou, bring order to foreign territories, and ultimately have a greater impact than if he had done otherwise.¹¹

For further elaboration on the notion of nonaction, one can return to the aforementioned passage from "Surveying Obscurities" of the *Huainanzi*. After the statement about *yexing*, the discussion continues:

故卻走馬以糞，而車軌不接於遠方之外，是謂坐馳陸沈，晝冥宵明，以冬鑠膠，以夏造冰。¹²

> Thus he retires his fast horses so they only make dung, and his chariot tracks do not need to extend beyond far-off lands. This is what is called racing while sitting, sinking in water on dry land, darkness at noon, bright light at night, melting pitch in winter, making ice in summer.

Here, the discussion introduces several additional expressions to complement the notion of *yexing*. These include *zuo chi* 坐馳 ("racing while sitting") and *lu chen* 陸沈 ("sinking in water on dry land"), all oxymorons like *yexing*.¹³ Whereas *yexing* describes an activity during a time of rest, with *zuo chi* and *lu chen* one is literally able to move without moving and sink without sinking. And more contradictions abound in the reminder of the same passage. By thwarting expectations and turning upside down the laws of nature, these expressions attest to some of the most marvelous powers of nonaction.¹⁴

The notion of nonaction can also be found in "All Things Flow into Form." The following statement describes how one is able to know the world without leaving home, or even one's seat (slip 29):

坐而思之，每 (謀) 於千里；记 (起) 而用之，練 (陳) 於四海 (海)。

Reflecting while one is seated, one plans what is a thousand miles away. Getting to action as one arises, one displays it to the four seas.

This corresponds to the paragraph immediately preceding this one (slips 14–17):

戠 (察) 道，坐不下筥 (席)；耑 (端) 曼 (冕)，箸 (圖) 不𢆶 (舉) 事，之〈先〉晢 (知) 四海 (海)，至聖 (聽) 千里，達見百里。是古 (故) 聖人原〈尻 (處)〉於丌 (其) 所，邦家 (家) 之厄 (危) 伕 (安) 鹰 (存) 忘 (亡)、惻 (賊) 懲 (盜) 之复 (作)，可之〈先〉晢 (知)。

Discerning the Way, one sits and does not descend from the sitting mat. Wearing the dark sacrificial robe and cap, one makes plans and needs not involve himself in actual affairs. One knows about the four seas ahead of others, having his hearing extend a thousand miles, and having his vision reach a hundred miles. Thus, while the sage resides in his home, he is able to know ahead of others the state's perils and prospects, the insurgence of thieves and robbers.

In its description of the sage's nonaction, "All Things Flow into Form" employs such hyperboles as "being seated without descending from the mat" (*zuo bu xia xi* 坐不下席) and "residing in one's home" (*chu yu qi suo* 處於其所) to emphasize the sage's fixture in one place. As for the expression *duanmian* 端冕 ("to wear the dark sacrificial robe and cap"), this is attested in the literary record as a ritual attire, much in the same way that *chuigong* 垂

拱, another commonly seen expression, denotes a respectful gesture: letting one's robes fall and folding the hands across the chest (as one leans forward slightly). The key, of course, is that both the gesture and the garment are merely display, involving no real action. As described by "All Things Flow into Form," the sage is able to put on this appearance and somehow still manages to know practically everything in the empire, ranging from state affairs at the topmost level to such mundane matters as the whereabouts of petty thieves.

The ideal of the ruler's nonaction is described in various ancient texts. Recall from chapter 3 the text from the *Book of Lord Shang* called "Charting the Policies" (Hua ce), with the statement: 是以人主處匡床之上, 聽絲竹之聲, 而天下治 "Hence, the ruler rests on a comfortable bed and listens to the sounds of musical instruments made of silk and bamboo, and the world is well ordered."[15] More interesting is the *Laozi* chapter 47: 不出戶, 可以知天下; 不窺牖, 可以見天道 "Without stirring abroad one can know the whole world; without looking out of the window one can see the way of heaven," followed by an explicit reference to the sage's nonaction: 是以聖人不行而知, 不見而明, 不為而成 "Therefore the sage knows without having to stir, identifies without having to see, accomplishes without having to act."[16] Another example is Xunzi's discussion in "Dispelling Blindness" (Jie bi) about the mind and its capacity to know everything in the world:

坐於室而見四海, 處於今而論久遠, 疏觀萬物而知其情, 參稽治亂而通其度, 經緯天地而材官萬物, 制割大理而宇宙裏矣 。

By sitting in his own house, a person can perceive all within the four seas. By living in the present, he can put in its proper place what is remote in space and distant in time. By penetrating into and inspecting the myriad things, he knows their essential qualities. By examining and testing order and disorder, he is fully conversant with their inner laws. By laying out the warp and woof of heaven and earth, he tailors the functions of the myriad things. By regulating and distinguishing according to the great ordering principle, he encompasses everything in space and time.[17]

Finally, we may consider the *Spring and Autumn Annals of Master Yan* (Yanzi chunqiu 晏子春秋), with the following remark attributed to Confucius: 夫不出于尊俎之間, 而知衝千里之外, 其晏子之謂也, 可謂折衝矣, 而太師其與焉 "Without leaving the vessels for food and drink and yet acting as a buffer a thousand *li* away, this is Yanzi. This can be called *zhe chong* ['acting as a buffer'], indeed! And the grand master also took part in this."[18] Once again, there is the notion that someone in a high position of power is able to exert influence without physically leaving his place. Here "the vessels of food and drink" (*zunzu* 尊俎; literally, cups and cutting boards for meat) refer to the banquet where Yanzi 晏子, working in tandem with the "grand master" (*taishi* 太師), pushes back several attempts by a foreign emissary to undermine his ruler, standing his ground against any infringement that could pave the way to a full-scale invasion. What I would like to dwell on, however, is a seemingly minor detail that I believe points to a basic feature about many of the discussions about nonaction.

As an alert reader might have already noticed in the passage from the *Spring and Autumn Annals of Master Yan*, there is a phrase: 可謂折衝矣 "This can be called *zhe chong* ['acting as a buffer'], indeed!" which follows upon and repeats the immediately preceding phrase about Yanzi: 夫不出于尊俎 之間, 而知衝千里之外 "Without leaving the vessels of food and drink and yet acting as a buffer a thousand *li* away." Although some scholars believe that the text is corrupt and would recommend deleting *kewei zhechong yi*, Shi Guangying 石光瑛 (1880–1943) suggests otherwise.[19] According to Shi, the first phrase about the vessels is actually an ancient saying, cited by Confucius, whereas *kewei zhechong yi* is Confucius's own observation, affirming that Yanzi has embodied this ideal. Thus, the two phrases are simply two overlapping comments made under different circumstances. As for the difference between *zhi* 知 (*tre) and *zhe* 折 (*tet), Shi follows previous scholars in suggesting that the former is simply a variant of the latter—literally, "to break."

These observations by Shi Guangying, if correct, point to an important feature of the passage from the *Spring and Autumn Annals of Master Yan*: the statement that describes the ideal of nonaction is a maxim much like "Return to the observance of the rites through overcoming oneself" (*ke ji fu li*), as discussed in chapter 3. Then, too, as is the case with that pithy saying from the *Analects* 12.1, this adage was inherited by Confucius, who followed it with his own comment. No wonder statements resembling this one appear in many other ancient texts and involve other interlocuters, since a common saying such as this, without any particular "source," would have been readily adapted by various authors. The same can be said about the notion of nonaction discussed in connection with it: rather than trying to pinpoint its origin and trace it to any particular thinker or textual source, it is more interesting to ask how it was used and what different contexts it appeared in. Based on my quick and partial survey of the large number of sources discussing this notion, the topics surrounding nonaction range from self-introspection and sincerity to the minimization of one's desires, empathetic understanding of others, the mystery surrounding the ruler, his role in setting a standard for the people, and the employment of worthy men, among others. This variety suggests a rich and multilayered background for us in considering the notion of *yexing*.

With this in place, we may now turn to the focus of the present chapter, a passage from Xunzi's essay "Dispelling Blindness" (Jie bi):

凡觀物有疑, 中心不定, 則外物不清; 吾慮不清, 則未可定然否也。冥冥而行者, 見寢石以為伏虎也, 見植林以為後人也, 冥冥蔽其明也。醉者越百步之溝, 以為蹞步之澮也, 俯而出城門, 以為小之閨也, 酒亂其神也。厭目而視者, 視一以為兩, 掩耳而聽者, 聽漠漠而以為啕啕, 埶亂其官也。故從山上望牛者若羊, 而求羊者不下牽也, 遠蔽其大也; 從山下望木者, 十仞之木若箸, 而求箸者不上折也, 高蔽其長也。水動而景搖, 人不以定美惡, 水埶玄也。瞽者仰視而不見星, 人不以定有無, 用精惑也。有人焉, 以此時定物, 則世之愚者也。彼愚者之定物, 以疑決疑, 決必不當。夫茍不當, 安能無過乎?

夏首之南有人焉, 曰涓蜀梁, 其為人也, 愚而善畏。明月而宵行, 俯見其影, 以為伏鬼也; 卬視其髮, 以為立魅也; 背而走, 比至其家者, 失氣而死, 豈不哀哉! 凡人之有鬼也, 必以其感忽之閒、疑玄之時正之。此人之所以無有而有無之時也, 而已以正事。故傷於溼而擊鼓鼓痺, 則必有敝鼓喪豚之費矣, 而未有俞疾之福也。故雖不在夏首之南, 則無以異矣。[20]

As a general rule, when examining things about which there are doubts, if the mind is not inwardly settled, then external things will not be clear. If my reflections are not clear, then I will never be able to settle what is so of a thing and what is not so of it. Someone walking along a road in the dark may see a fallen stone and think it a tiger crouching in ambush, or he may see upright trees and think there are people behind them. The darkness has beclouded the clarity of his vision. A drunk may jump across a ditch a hundred paces wide, thinking it a drain half a pace wide, or may stoop down to go out the city gate, thinking it a small doorway. The drink has disordered his spirit. Press against the eye while looking at an object will make it appear double;

covering the ears when listening will make silence seem like a clamor. The force applied to the sense organs has disordered them. Hence, looking down at oxen from the top of a mount will make them appear the size of a sheep, but someone looking for sheep will not go down to lead them away. The distance has obscured their true size. If from the foot of a mountain you look up at a tree, a tree ten *ren* high looks like a chopstick, but someone looking for chopsticks would not climb up to break it off. The height has obscured its true length. When water is moving and reflections waver, men do not use it to determine their beauty or ugliness. The circumstances of the water make for deception. A blind man tilting his head back and looking up will not see the stars; so men do not have him determine whether there are stars or not. The essential vigor of his eyes is impaired. If there were anyone who would use occasions such as these to determine the nature of things, then he would be the biggest fool in the world. Such a fool's determination of things uses what is doubtful to judge doubtful points. The judging would of necessity be invalid. And if indeed his judging is invalid, how can he not err?

South of the head of the Xia River there was a man named Juan Shuliang. He was a foolish man who was prone to fright. One evening when the moon was bright, he was out walking when he looked down and saw his own shadow, which he took to be a crouching ghost. Raising his head, he caught sight of his own hair and took it to be an ogre standing over him. He turned his back and raced away. Just when he reached his house, he lost his *qi* vital breath and died. Alas, what a shame! As a general rule, when men think there are ghosts, the judgment is certain to take place on an occasion when they are startled or confused. This is an occasion when these men, in taking what does not exist for what does and what does exist for what does not, proceed to decide a matter. Hence, if a person affected by dampness beats a drum to drive away the rheumatism, he is certain to pay the cost of wearing out a drum and losing a pig, but he will never have the blessing of being cured of his illness. Thus, although he does not live to the south of the head of the Xia River, there is no difference between him and the man who did.

Xunzi begins this discussion by stating a problem that afflicts the mind and affects its capacity to observe the world at large: 凡觀物有疑, 中心不定, 則外物不清; 吾慮不清, 則未可定然否也 "As a general rule, when examining things about which there are doubts, if the mind is not inwardly settled, then external things will not be clear. If my reflections are not clear, then I will never be able to settle what is so of a thing and what is not so of it." Such a problem stems from the mind's being "unsettled" (*buding* 不定), and the uncertainty only grows as one applies the mind to make further decisions, or "using what is doubtful to judge doubtful points" (*yi yi jue yi* 以疑決疑). The result? "The judging would of necessity be invalid" (*jue bi bu dang* 決必不當). And this is followed by Xunzi's rhetorical question that concludes the first part of the passage: 夫苟不當, 安能無過乎 "If indeed his judging is invalid, how can he not err?"

Among the examples that Xunzi uses to make his point in this passage, there is the illusion of a crouching tiger as observed by someone who *mingming er xing* 冥冥而行 ("walks along a road in the dark").[21] Such a description of walking by night must be Xunzi's focus, since he returns to it in the second half of the passage, in the parable of a man named Juan Shuliang 涓蜀梁, and he ends his discussion with a reference to "south of the head of the Xia River" (*Xiashou zhi nan* 夏首之南), where Juan Shuliang resides. Regarding this man, Xunzi describes in some detail the predicament that stems from his internal confusion. Walking alone one night, the man is startled by his own shadow and his own hair, mistaking them for ghosts and ogres. Trying to rid himself of these creatures, he runs until he is out of breath, collapses, and dies. As Xunzi sums up the significance of the parable: 此人之所以無有而有無之時也, 而已以正事 "This is an occasion when these men, in taking what does not exist for what does and what does exist for what does not, proceed to decide a matter."[22] For Xunzi, Juan Shuliang epitomizes the futility of engaging with the outside world when one is not completely right in the head.

Probing deeper into Xunzi's criticism of Juan Shuliang, it seems to me that for this "foolish man who was prone to fright" to mistake his shadow and hair for ghosts and ogres, the basic fallacy is that he identifies agency where it does not belong, as if the various integral parts of oneself all of a sudden took on lives of their own. That is to say, Juan Shuliang's predicament stems from an inability to recognize himself as only himself, not many persons. Compare this with the man who mistakes a rock for a tiger. In this case, the confusion is not over oneself (mistaking what belongs to oneself with what does not) but over the external landscape (mistaking one element for another). Both are due to the mind's being "unsettled," or "taking what does not exist for what does and what does exist for what does not" (*yi wu you er you wu* 以無有而有無).

Based on this understanding of Juan Shuliang's parable, I would connect it with an earlier passage in "Dispelling Blindness" where Xunzi describes the harm caused by leaving the mind unattended: 心, 臥則夢, 偷則自行, 使之則謀 "The mind dreams when it lies down, moves of its own accord when it relaxes, and plans when it is employed."[23] Here, regarding *xing* 行 ("to move"), one will recognize immediately that it is the same word as *xing* in *yexing* ("walking by night"). More importantly, with *wo ze meng* 臥則夢 ("it dreams when it lies down"—an activity that usually takes place at night), this earlier passage of "Dispelling Blindness" describes a situation where thoughts arise on their own in an unmonitored manner. If unchecked, they may lead to various follies and improper schemes, which would ultimately lead the mind astray. Thus, I understand Juan Shuliang's parable to be a dramatic representation of this earlier statement. Whether one is dreaming or walking by night and being blinded by darkness, the confusion is the same. If, in such a state of confusion, the mind or a part of it can wander off on its own, then of course it can also come back as a ghost or ogre and haunt one to death.[24]

In the overall context of "Dispelling Blindness," the topic that Xunzi repeatedly emphasizes is the oneness of the mind: singular, unified, and one. This is explicitly stated in the opening statement of the text, where Xunzi suggests that the cause of bias is a person's having two minds as opposed to just one: 凡人之患, 蔽於一曲而闇於大理; 治則復經, 兩疑則惑矣; 天下無二道, 聖人無兩心 "It is the common flaw of men to be blinded by some small detail and to neglect the great ordering principle. If cured of this flaw, they can return to the classical standard, but if they remain with double principles, they will stay suspicious and deluded.[25] The world does not have two ways, and the sage is not of two minds." The same idea is repeated at the end of the first part of the text, before Xunzi proceeds to single out Juan Shuliang and another thinker for more extensive criticism: 自古及今, 未嘗有兩而能精者也 "From antiquity until the present day there has never been anyone that was of two minds who was able to concentrate on a single purpose."

The notion of Oneness is also addressed elsewhere in "Dispelling Blindness." In one memorable passage, Xunzi asks the rhetorical question:

人何以知道 "What do men use to know the way?" His response: 心 "The mind." This is followed by another question: 心何以知 "How does the mind know?" To which he replies: 虛壹而靜 "By its emptiness, unity, and stillness." Later in the text, the term *yi* 壹 is defined as follows: 心生而有知, 知而有異, 異也者, 同時兼知之; 同時兼知之, 兩也, 然而有所謂一, 不以夫一害此一, 謂之壹 "The mind from birth has awareness. Having awareness, there is perception of difference. Perception of difference consists in awareness of two aspects of things at the same time. Awareness of two aspects of things all at the same time entails duality. Nonetheless the mind has the quality called unity. Not allowing the one thing to interfere with the other is called unity." It is on this basis that Xunzi immediately proceeds to discuss the problem of the mind's leading itself astray, as previously cited.[26]

If, at this point, we turn from "Dispelling Blindness" to "All Things Flow into Form," we may read the two texts against each other. Recall "the heart of hearts" formulation, stated at the beginning of the passage from "All Things Flow into Form":

> It has been said that if the mind does not prevail over the mind, then great chaos arises; if the mind can prevail over the mind, this is called "arriving in the morning." What is meant by "arriving in the morning"? That one reveals oneself for inspection by others. How is it known that one has revealed himself? That one will be at ease with himself for all his life.

On the surface, this formulation could not appear more different from Xunzi's ideal as revealed in "Dispelling Blindness." Whereas "All Things Flow into Form" and other related texts envision a mind with multiple constituents, Xunzi holds that it is one. But a closer look suggests that they are actually quite similar. "All Things Flow into Form" wants to rid the mind of harmful influences, so an innermost core could be preserved and quarantined. This results in a certain state of personal freedom, or *zhongshen zi ruo* ("one will be at ease with himself for all his life"). By contrast, Xunzi warns against the neglect of one's mind, pointing to the potential of thoughts running out of control and leading the mind astray, or as he puts it, *tou ze zi xing* 偷則自行 ("The mind moves of its own accord when it relaxes"). The similarity of the two phrases betrays the fact that they are coming at each other from opposite directions. In one instance, a person is incapacitated by a mind that has not been properly cultivated, and he simply gives up. In the other, he successfully makes it to the other side and rests assured of his hard-won battle. In the end, for both texts, there is only one mind, if attended the right way.

In light of this connection, we can see that the notion of Oneness is also critical to "All Things Flow into Form." Consider the rhetorical questions that serve to define the expression *xiao cheng*: 能寡言乎? 能一乎? 夫此之謂削成 "Is one capable of speaking few words? Capable of being One? This is called 'the paring down of what is completed.'" I will have more to say about this in the final chapter of the study. For the moment, we might simply note the emphasis on Oneness that is made more generally in the remainder of the same passage: "It is said: it is only the ruler that the hundred clans value. It is only the mind that the ruler values. It is only One that the mind values. If it gets to be released, then upward it fills up heaven, and downward it coils up in the abyss. Reflecting while one is seated, one plans what is a thousand miles away. Getting to action as one arises, one displays it to the four seas." As the discussion narrows, first from the people to the ruler, then from the various constituents of the ruler's physical form to his mind, and finally to the principle of Oneness, it is clear that Oneness is at the very heart of "All Things Flow into Form." The passage goes on to describe how such a principle permeates everywhere and everything in the world, using a formulaic language shared by several other ancient texts.[27]

There is another reason for reading "Dispelling Blindness" and "All Things Flow into Form" side by side, which will be discussed in chapter 5, but it should be clear from the brief analysis here that much of Xunzi's discussion, including his parable of the man frightened by his own hair and shadow, is based on a conception of the mind also shared by "All Things Flow into Form." Although Xunzi is critical of this conception, I believe he also agrees with it on many points. This includes the emphasis on the notion of Oneness (or a single mind), the topic at the heart of "Dispelling Blindness" that is also repeatedly seen in "All Things Flow into Form." Thus, I would account for this somewhat inconsistent picture by suggesting that Xunzi was criticizing a teaching while adopting it as his own, the kind of move that is also evident elsewhere in "Dispelling Blindness," as I argue in another work.[28] While the possibility remains that Xunzi was drawing a finer distinction between himself and his predecessors, a simpler explanation is that he was simply being unfair to them. Needless to say, such a conclusion does not diminish the value of the accounts that Xunzi has left behind. But a painstaking analysis of sources inaccessible to earlier scholars enables us to have a fuller understanding of the targets of Xunzi's criticisms—not as the parodic stick figures that he makes them out to be, but actual thinkers in competition with him.

In the remainder of this chapter, I will consider in some detail the identity of the person who is frightened by his own shadow, Juan Shuliang. Starting with the surname, one can note that Juan 涓 is from the same phonetic series as Yuan 蜎 (*ʔwên), and it is nearly homophonous with Huan 環 (*wên). As for Shuliang 蜀梁, *shu* 蜀 is from the same phonetic series as *du* 獨, and the reading of Duliang 獨梁 "a single log" implies a situation of precariousness that calls for further explanation. Consider the following aphorism from the text in the *Huainanzi* called "Profound Precepts" (Miucheng): 不自遁, 斯亦不遁人; 故若行獨梁, 不為無人不兢其容 "If you do not deceive yourself, you will not deceive others. It is like crossing a bridge made from a single log. Just because there is no one else present does not mean you do not exhibit a cautious look."[29] A man who walks on a single log feels afraid regardless of whether he is watched by others. Here, the word *jing* 兢 ("to look cautious") is the verbal form of *jingjing* 兢兢 ("cautious"), most famously attested in "The Lesser Severity" (Xiaomin 小旻), a poem of the *Book of Odes*: 戰戰兢兢, 如臨深淵, 如履薄冰 "Trembling and cautious, as if approaching a deep abyss, as if treading on thin ice."[30] Note that one of the two situations given in this line is the *shenyuan* 深淵 ("deep abyss"), which corresponds to *duliang* ("a single log") from "Profound Precepts" in the sense that a single log is precisely what traverses a deep abyss, and it inspires little confidence in the person who is crossing. Now, if one took the word *yuan* 淵 and combined it with Huan 環, the result would be Huan Yuan 環淵, an obscure thinker of the Warring States who is nevertheless attested in the literary record.[31]

The references to Huan Yuan in the literary record are few and far between. Whereas the *Grand Scribe's Records* identifies him as Huan Yuan, the *History of the Former Han* (Hanshu 漢書) mentions an eponymous work called the *Yuanzi* 蜎子, with the appended note that his proper name is Yuan 淵.[32] Among the various ancient traditions about this figure, the ones related to his name Yuan are the most interesting for our purpose. In addition to the meaning of "abyss," the word can also mean "origin." In both cases, it denotes a location where fish gather (as opposed to the shallow waters, where they are more clearly visible to fishermen and thus more easily caught).[33] This is no doubt why many references to Huan Yuan in the literary record concern his expertise in fishing.[34] One catches only a glimpse of this lore in "Dispelling Blindness," where Juan Shuliang is associated with the location "south of the head of the Xia River" (*Xiashou zhi nan*).[35]

In discussing these matters, I assume that a name such as Huan Yuan is reflective of stories about the same figure: a name might have inspired legends, just as legends could have given rise to a name. This is by no means an isolated phenomenon and can be seen in the stories about Confucius, Mozi 墨子, and other renowned ancient figures. Although such stories are often interpreted by scholars as efforts to mythologize the figure concerned, I believe the reverse is also possible: some personal details may have come about due to these stories. For one example parallel to Huan Yuan, consider the legends about Laozi 老子 collected in his biography in the *Grand Scribe's Records*, particularly the episode that Laozi left behind a work of five thousand characters with a director at a pass (*guan lingyin* 關令尹). Most readers of this episode have connected this figure with a Guan Yin 關尹 mentioned together with Laozi in the text in the *Annals of Lü Buwei* called "No Duality" (Bu er 不二) and the text in the *Zhuangzi* called "The World" (Tianxia 天下), even though neither of these sources mentions his gatekeeping duty or the encounter with Laozi. It seems to me that the uncertainty surrounding this mysterious figure is similar to that in Huan Yuan's case; one cannot be sure whether it was the name Guan Yin that led to the detail about his duty or the duty that gave the man his name.[36]

But it is to the aphorism from "Profound Precepts" of the *Huainanzi* that I want to return, since I believe this contains one of the most critical details about the identity of Juan Shuliang. According to this text, the fear of crossing a precarious bridge has nothing to do with the presence of others. Acknowledging one's true feeling reflects a genuineness of character that is both *bu zi dun* 不自遁 ("not deceiving himself") and *bu dun ren* 不遁人 ("not deceiving others"). Here, the emphasis is on oneself, and the absence of others implies that one is alone. Such a moment of self-scrutiny is exactly what one finds in the various discussions of walking by night. Just as one must cross a precarious bridge regardless of whether one is being watched, a virtuous man such as King Wen (to use the example cited at the beginning of this chapter) will carry out good deeds whether he is recognized or not. Of course, an expression such as *bu zi dun* ("not deceiving himself") also echoes *zi ruo* ("being at ease with oneself") in "All Things Flow into Form." A person is himself only if he faces up to his true feeling with no self-delusion.

If these connections are valid, then the name of Juan Shuliang, the traditions surrounding it, and the situations described in those traditions all point to the same figure. To the extent that these sources are related to "All Things Flow into Form" and the discussions of walking by night tied to it, they enable one to understand more precisely the nature of Xunzi's comments in the "Dispelling Blindness." Huan Yuan, which I believe is simply a variant form of Juan Shuliang, may have been the figure that Xunzi identified as responsible for all of the teachings reviewed in this chapter.

Finally, it is noteworthy that the various forms in which Juan Shuliang's surname is attested, whether Juan 涓, Yuan 蜎 (*ʔwên), or Huan 環 (*wên), are all related in sound to another word, *qiong* 煢 (*gweŋ) or "alone," as discussed in chapter 1. Evidence of such interchange can be found under "Solitary Pyrus Tree" (Didu 杕杜), a poem from the *Odes*: 獨行睘睘, 豈無他人 "Alone I walk and helpless; are there no other people?"[37] As noted by Lu Deming 陸德明 (556–627), the character *qiong* 睘 (from the same phonetic series as *huan* 環) has the variant of *qiong* 煢 and *qiong* 㷀. Interestingly, "Solitary Pyrus Tree" contains another line similar to the one just cited: 獨行踽踽, 豈無他人 "Alone I walk and forlorn; are there no other people?" Here the word *juju* 踽踽 ("forlorn") appears in a position parallel to *qiongqiong* 睘睘 ("helpless") and is closely related in its meaning. Note that *ju* 踽 is from the same phonetic series as *ju* 偊, seen earlier in Nüju 女偊, the main interlocutor of the passage from "The Great and Venerable Teacher" of the *Zhuangzi*, discussed also in chapter 1. This suggests that the name Nüju, just like Juan Shuliang, is not accidental. In both cases, the name is closely interfused with the notion of solitary walking, whether such walking takes place at night or over a precarious bridge.[38] Recall the question from "The Great and Venerable Teacher," posed by Nanbo Zikui to Nüju: 子獨惡乎聞之 "How is it that you alone heard about this?" Now *du* ("alone") takes on an additional layer of meaning, one that befits Nüju's name.

CHAPTER 5

One

As mentioned in chapter 4, the notion of Oneness is central to both Xunzi's essay "Dispelling Blindness" and "All Things Flow into Form." For the latter text, in particular, Oneness is evoked in connection with the expression *xiao cheng*: 能寡言乎? 能一乎? 夫此之謂削成 "Is one capable of speaking few words? Capable of being One? This is called 'the paring down of what is completed.'" And the discussion follows with the elaboration: 百姓之所貴唯君, 君之所貴唯心, 心之所貴唯一 "It is only the ruler that the hundred clans value. It is only the mind that the ruler values. It is only One that the mind values." This is the focus of the present chapter, which considers several ancient accounts that share with "All Things Flow into Form" not only the same interest in the notion of Oneness but also the same rhetorical formula. One of these accounts is a text from the *Zhuangzi* called "Gengsang Chu" (a passage different from the one examined in chapter 2), which contains a crucial piece of evidence that confirms the comparison of "Dispelling Blindness" and "All Things Flow into Form" such as I attempted in chapter 4.

We may begin with chapter 10 of the *Laozi*:

載營魄抱一, 能無離乎? 專氣致柔, 能若嬰兒乎? 滌除玄覽, 能無疵乎? 愛民治國, 能無以知乎? 天門開闔, 能為雌乎? 明白四達, 能無以為乎? 生之畜之, 生而不有, 為而不恃, 長而不宰, 是謂玄德。[1]

When you envelop your bodily soul and embrace Oneness, can you not let go?[2] In concentrating your breath and bringing about suppleness, can you be as a babe? Can you polish your mysterious mirror and leave no blemish? Can you love the people and govern the state without knowing anything? When the gates of heaven open and shut, are you capable of keeping to the role of the female? When your discernment penetrates the four quarters, are you capable of not doing anything? It gives them life and rears them. It gives them life yet claims no possession. It benefits them yet exacts no gratitude; it is the steward yet exercises no authority. Such is called the mysterious virtue.

Here, in emphasizing the importance of *bao yi* 抱一 ("embracing Oneness"), the discussion poses a series of rhetorical questions that underscore the same notion of nonaction that we saw in chapter 4. Can the ruler govern the state and oversee his realm without knowing and doing anything? This echoes the comparison with a baby, which one should imitate, and the passive female, which one should embody. Such is the "mysterious virtue" (*xuande* 玄德) that concludes the discussion, and it corresponds to an inner "mysterious mirror" (*xuanlan* 玄覽) earlier in the passage, where *xuan* 玄 ("mysterious") is literally "dark" or "obscure," like King Wen the Zhou founder carrying about in secret, or *yinxing*. As one will see shortly, such conception of darkness or obscurity is critical for understanding a passage from "All Things Flow into Form."

A second passage to consider is the "Sixteen Canons" (Shiliujing 十六經) from the silk manuscripts discovered at the Han tomb in Mawangdui. In a section called "Compliance with the Way" (Shun dao 順道), there is the following discussion (lines 64a–65a):

欲知得失, 請必審名察刑 (形)。刑 (形) 恆自定, 是我俞 (愈) 靜; 事恆自㐌 (施), 是我无為。靜翳 (噎) 不動, 來自至, 去自往。能一乎? 能止乎? 能毋有己, 能自擇而奠 (尊) 理乎? 紆 (紓) 也, 屯也, 丌 (其) 如莫存。萬物群至, 我无不能應。我不臧 (藏) 故, 不挾陳。鄉 (向) 者已去, 至者乃新。新故不翏 (繆), 我有所周。[3]

If you desire to know about gain and loss, you must please investigate names fully and to examine into forms. Forms constantly determine themselves, and for this reason I am more at rest. Affairs constantly manage themselves: for this reason I do not act. Be at rest, quiet, and do not move: what comes, arrives by itself; what goes, departs by itself. Can you be one? Can you stop? Can you be without a self? Can you make selections on your own and honor a sense of inherent order? Protect and accumulate it as though it did not exist.[4] When the myriad things come flocking together, I cannot but respond. I do not store the old; I do not clasp the stale. The past is already gone; what comes is new. The new and the old are not to be intermingled: I encompass everything everywhere.

Again, this discussion is centered on the notion of nonaction, as can be seen in the statement: 形恆自定, 是我愈靜; 事恆自施, 是我无為 "Forms constantly determine themselves, and for this reason I am more at rest. Affairs constantly manage themselves: for this reason I do not act." This describes an ideal where I keep myself at a distance from things and allow them to run their course. It is followed by a series of rhetorical questions that resemble both chapter 10 of the *Laozi* and "All Things Flow into Form": 能一乎? 能止乎? 能毋有己, 能自擇而尊理乎 "Can you be one? Can you stop? Can you be without a self? Can you make selections on your own and honor a sense of inherent order?" Here *zi ze* 自擇 ("to make selections on one's own") is the choosing of some things over others, and the basis for this is "honoring a sense of inherent order" (*zun li* 尊理), or adhering to the set of patterns that permeate all things. This enables me to act with the same naturalness and spontaneity as implied by the term *zi ruo* ("to be at ease with oneself") from "All Things Flow into Form."[5] For "Sixteen Canons," I am able to manage all things in this way: 萬物群至, 我无不能應 "When the myriad things come flocking together, I cannot but respond." Things do not get confused, and I am able to provide for them all: 新故不繆, 我有所周 "The new and the old are not to be intermingled: I encompass everything everywhere."

For a parallel to "Sixteen Canons," we may turn to the text from the *Guanzi* called "Art of the Mind, Part Two" (Xinshu xia), which describes the same ideals of nonaction as the following:

一氣能變曰精, 一事能變曰智。纂[6]選者所以等事也, 極變者所以應物也。纂選而不亂, 極變而不煩, 執一之君子。[7]

What is at one with the vital force and able to bring about changes in it is called the vital essence. What is at one with affairs and is able to bring about changes in them is called wisdom. To make selections is the way to establish priorities in affairs. Being extremely flexible is the way to respond to things.

> To make selections without becoming confused, to be extremely flexible without creating trouble—only the gentleman who grasps the One is able to do this.

According to this discussion, the gentleman concentrates his *qi* (vital force), maintains his focus, and thus takes care of all things by allotting them to their proper places. This defines the gentleman's *zhi yi* 執一 ("grasping Oneness"), which of course corresponds to *bao yi* 抱一 ("embracing Oneness") from the *Laozi*. The discussion continues with this elaboration: 執一而不失, 能君萬物, 日月之與同光, 天地之與同理 "Grasping the One and never losing it, he is able to become prince over all things. His brightness is on a par with the sun and the moon. His sense of inherent order is on a par with Heaven and Earth." Here, we encounter the same "sense of inherent order" (*li* 理) mentioned in "Sixteen Canons." It is what underlies the operation of Oneness in both of these texts. In light of these parallels, it perhaps comes as little surprise that "Art of the Mind, Part Two" begins its discussion with a series of rhetorical questions resembling many of the texts examined in this chapter: 能專乎? 能一乎? 能毋卜筮而知凶吉乎? 能止乎? 能已乎? 能毋問於人而自得之於己乎? "Can you concentrate? Can you focus? Without resorting to tortoise shell and milfoil, can you foretell bad fortune from good? Can you tell where to stop? Can you tell when to desist? Rather than asking others, can you find it within yourself?"

"Art of the Mind, Part Two" has a close connection with another text from the *Guanzi*, "Inner Workings" (Neiye). In fact, as we saw in chapter 3, both of these texts contain "the heart of hearts" formulation: 心之中又有心 "Within the mind there is another mind."[8] In discussing "the manifestations of the mind and the vital forces" (*xinqi zhi xing* 心氣之形), this second text from the *Guanzi* observes that the vital forces, as dictated by the mind, are the key to a spirit-like power: 搏[9]氣如神, 萬物備存 "If you concentrate your vital force until you become like the spirit, your grasp of all things will be complete." This is followed, once again, by a series of rhetorical questions: 能搏[10]乎? 能一乎? 能無卜筮而知凶吉[11]乎? 能止乎? 能已乎? 能勿求諸人而得[12]之己乎? "Can you concentrate? Can you focus? Without resorting to tortoise shell and milfoil, can you foretell bad fortune from good? Can you tell where to stop? Can you tell when to desist? Rather than seeking it in others, can you find it within yourself?" Besides the parallel with the expression *zi ruo* from "All Things Flow into Form," as already discussed, we should note that in its description of the cultivation of an inner vital essence (*jing*), "Inner Workings" speaks of a glowing light that contrasts with what is internal to oneself: 精存自生, 其外安榮 "When the vital essence is present, it naturally produces life, and outwardly it produces a restful glow." This draws a further connection with "All Things Flow into Form," particularly the discussion of the transparency of one's intentions, as we saw in chapter 2.[13]

In both texts from the *Guanzi*, the rhetorical questions mention divination and the prediction of the future, contrasting these mantic arts with the principle of Oneness. The sense is that if I am able to grasp the principle of Oneness, then the insights about the cosmos that I gain consequently would allow me to navigate my way in this world in a manner that the mantric arts cannot. This is critical not only for understanding the "Gengsang Chu" from the *Zhuangzi*, which I will discuss shortly, but also for drawing out a feature of "All Things Flow into Form."

The passage from "Gengsang Chu" that I would like to examine is roughly divided into two sections.[14] The first features an exchange between the eponymous figure and his disciples, particularly Nanrong Chu 南榮趎. The second records the effort by the same disciple to seek out further instruction from none other than Laozi. There is some indication that this text was part of a broader tradition about Nanrong Chu's quest for wisdom, reflected in several ancient sources. Much is of interest, but for my purpose, I will single out only a couple of points.

The first concerns the initial instruction from Gengsang Chu to Nanrong Chu: 全汝形, 抱汝生, 无使汝思慮營營 "Keep the body whole, cling fast to life. Do not fall prey to the fidget and fuss of thoughts and scheming." In response to this, the disciple remains skeptical:

目之與形, 吾不知其異也, 而盲者不能自見; 耳之與形, 吾不知其異也, 而聾者不能自聞; 心之與形, 吾不知其異也, 而狂者不能自得。形之與形亦辟矣, 而物或閒之邪? 欲相求而不能相得。今謂趎曰:「全汝形, 抱汝生, 無使汝思慮營營。」趎勉聞道達耳矣!

The eyes are part of the body—I have never thought them anything else—yet the blind man cannot see with his. The ears are part of the body—I have never thought them anything else—yet the deaf man cannot hear with his. The mind is part of the body—I have never thought it anything else—yet the madman cannot comprehend with his. The body too must be part of the body—surely they are intimately connected.[15] Yet—is it because something intervenes? I try to seek my body, but I cannot find it. Now you tell me, "Keep the body whole, cling fast to life! Do not fall prey to the fidget and fuss of thoughts and scheming." As hard as I try to understand your explanation of the Way, I'm afraid your words penetrate no farther than my ears.

For Nanrong Chu, the advice from his teacher is easier said than done. How is it possible to "keep the body whole" (*quan ruxing* 全汝形) when the multiple parts of the body have the potential to malfunction and thus affect one's capacity to "cling fast to life" (*bao rusheng* 抱汝生)? As Nanrong Chu continues: 形之與形亦辟矣，而物或閒之邪 "The body too must be part of the body—surely they are intimately connected. Yet—is it because something intervenes?" Notice that the formulation of this dilemma resembles "All Things Flow into Form" and other texts that share the conception of the "heart of hearts." Just as the mind might be divided, here Nanrong Chu mentions the possibility that the various parts of the body (i.e., eyes, ears, mind) could become fragmented due to the interference of certain "things" (*wu* 物). Such disintegration would be the opposite of what the teacher suggests about "keeping the body whole and clinging fast to life." Here Nanrong Chu's purpose is not so much to challenge his teacher as to indicate his continuing struggle with a problem that is perhaps all too common.[16]

In response to Nanrong Chu's question, the teacher throws up his hands and concedes that this is beyond his wits. He directs Nanrong Chu to see his own teacher, Laozi, and Nanrong Chu sets off on an arduous journey. Upon meeting Laozi, Nanrong Chu is initiated into a program of self-cultivation, and he eventually understands the significance of the earlier advice by Gengsang Chu. There is one part of this exchange that has a bearing on my discussion, but first I would like to draw attention to Laozi's words to Nanrong Chu upon receiving him: 子自楚之所來乎 "Did you come from [Gengsang] Chu's place?" Nanrong Chu replies in the affirmative. Laozi asks again: 子何與人偕來之眾也 "Why did you come with all this crowd of people?" To this, Nanrong Chu, "astonished, turned to look behind him" (*juran gu qi hou* 懼然顧其後). Notice the similarity between Laozi's comment and the parable about Juan Shuliang from Xunzi's "Dispelling Blindness." Both concern the predicament of a person whose lack of a unified, focused mind results in his inability to rein in the different parts of his *self*.[17] In Juan Shuliang's case, this is dramatized by the man's illusion that his shadow and hair have taken on lives of their own. In Nanrong Chu's case, these multiple agencies form a crowd discernible only to the sagacious Laozi. Such detail from "Gengsang Chu" attests to a common set of concerns that I believe also underlie "All Things Flow into Form" and "Dispelling Blindness," and it validates my decision to juxtapose and compare the two texts, as I attempted to do in the previous chapter.

In fact, when we look further into the body of lore surrounding Nanrong, we see more connections between this figure and the fable from "Dispelling Blindness," particularly the notion of a journey in the night. In a text from the *Wenzi* 文子 called "Pure Sincerity" (Jingcheng 精誠), Nanrong Chu is mentioned as an example of the perfect man: 至人潛行, 譬猶雷霆之藏也, 隨時而舉事, 因資而立功, 進退無難, 無所不通 "The perfect man acts under cover, like how thunder and lightning are hidden. He launches enterprises in accordance with the times, and achieves great accomplishments by what has been provided to him. He advances and withdraws without any difficulty, and there is nowhere he does not penetrate."[18] In a text from the *New Documents* (Xinshu 新書) called "An Exhortation to Learning" (Quanxue 勸學), there is also the account: 昔者南榮跦, 醜聖道之忘乎己, 故步涉山川, 蚤冒楚棘, 彌道千餘, 百舍重繭而不敢久息 "Nanrong Chu of the past imitated the way of the sages and forgot himself. So he walked over mountains and waded rivers, passed under thorns and brambles and covered thousands of roads. He lodged along the way for hundreds of nights and his feet were covered with calluses, and yet he dared not rest for too long."[19] In the first instance, *qianxing* ("acting under cover") is another form of *yexing* ("walking in the night"), as already pointed out in chapter 4. In the second instance, the suggestion that Nanrong Chu "forgot himself" (*wang hu ji* 忘乎己) betrays the theme of self-struggle that also underlies "Gengsang Chu." The only difference is that in the *New Documents*, our hero is so successful that he wipes out all traces of himself, or one might say it is after having gone through the process of self-cultivation recorded in "Gengsang Chu" that Nanrong Chu is able to forget himself in the *New Documents*. This is no more a contradiction than what we find in accounts about walking alone at night: darkness can confuse and benight a person (Juan Shuliang of Xunzi's "Dispelling Blindness") or it can sharpen one's attention and focus (the archer whose arrow penetrates a rock). All of these sources point to a common set of themes surrounding Nanrong Chu. This is visible also in "Gengsang Chu," even though in that text from the *Zhuangzi* he takes somewhat of a back seat vis-à-vis Gengsang Chu and Laozi.

Toward the end of "Gengsang Chu," we find Laozi commenting on the "basic rules of self-preservation" (*weisheng zhi jing* 衛生之經), in response to a request by Nanrong Chu. This is Laozi's explanation:

衛生之經, 能抱一乎? 能勿失乎? 能无卜筮而知凶吉[20]乎? 能止乎? 能已乎? 能舍諸人而求諸己乎? 能翛然乎? 能侗然乎? 能兒子乎? 兒子終日嗥而嗌不嗄, 和之至也; 終日握而手不掜, 共其德也; 終日視而目不瞚, 偏不在外也。行不知所之, 居不知所為, 與物委蛇, 而同其波。是衛生之經已。

With the basic rules of life-preservation, can you embrace Oneness? Can you keep from losing it? Can you, without tortoise shell or divining stalks, foretell fortune and misfortune? Do you know where to stop? Do you know where to leave off? Do you know how to disregard it in others and instead look for it in yourself? Can you be brisk and unflagging? Can you be rude and unwitting? Can you be a little baby? The baby howls all day, yet its throat never gets hoarse—harmony at its height! The baby makes fists all day, yet its fingers never get cramped—virtue is what it holds onto. The baby stares all day without blinking its eyes—it has no preferences in the world of externals. To move without knowing where you are going, to sit at home without knowing what you are doing, traipsing and trailing about with other things, riding along with them on the same wave, these are the basic rule of self-preservation, these and nothing more.

In reading this discussion, we immediately notice the series of rhetorical questions that bear such a close resemblance to many of the texts examined in this chapter: "All Things Flow into Form," "Sixteen Canons" from Mawangdui, the *Laozi* chapter 10, and the two texts from the *Guanzi*, "Inner Workings" and "Art of the Mind, Part Two." Indeed, as I mentioned earlier in regard to these last two texts, implicit in these rhetorical questions is an opposition between the principle of Oneness and divination. And we find the same opposition in "Gengsang Chu," though divination is now lumped together with another technical art, or what is called *weisheng zhi jing* ("basic rules of self-preservation").[21] On this topic, Laozi's remarks carry a somewhat critical undertone. After all, it was not Laozi's idea to engage in a discussion of these "basic rules of self-preservation," but Nangong Chu's.[22] This serious if also dim-witted novice had requested for Laozi to instruct him about a path that was suited to his limited understanding: 趎願聞衛生之經而已矣 "What I, Chu, would like to ask about are simply the basic rules of life-preservation, that is all." Notice the series of final particles translated by Watson as "simply . . . that is all," which signal Nangong Chu's extreme caution. By the time we get to Laozi's final statement: 是衛生之經已 "These are the basic rule of self-preservation, *these and nothing more*," it is clear that his remarks were in no way intended to expound on these second-rate teachings that Nanchong wished to learn about but a challenge against them—indeed, an attempt to redefine them. In the new formulation by Laozi, these teachings would be grounded in the principle of Oneness, and they would return one to a nascent state where one is simple, natural, and pure, just like an infant.[23]

If, at this point, we go back to Xunzi's "Dispelling Blindness," then it is perhaps unsurprising that given all the attention to the notion of Oneness in that text, there is also an attempt to diminish the importance of competing measures, in this case the offering of sacrifice and performance, which promise to influence the spirits and thus determine one's future just as much as divination has the potential to do so. This appears at the very end of the parable about Juan Shuliang:

故傷於溼而擊鼓鼓痺，則必有敝鼓喪豚之費矣，而未有俞疾之福也。

Hence, if a person affected by dampness beats a drum to drive away the rheumatism, he is certain to pay the cost of wearing out a drum and losing a pig, but he will never have the blessing of being cured of his illness.

In other words, for a physical ailment such as dampness or rheumatism, it does little good to seek help from the spirits; and here Xunzi's rationalism is unmistakable despite his never spelling out what other treatments one might take up instead. This is another example offered by "Dispelling Blindness" on the confusion between what is internal to oneself and what is not. As is consistent with "Gengsang Chu," Xunzi allocates to a secondary place any consideration of the supernatural, and he reserves his priority for the notion of Oneness that is at the heart of "Dispelling Blindness."

To end the discussion in this chapter, we may turn to the following passage from "All Things Flow into Form" (slips 15, 24, 25):

昏 (聞) 之曰: 至 (致) 情而智 (知), 戠 (察) 智 (知) 而神, 戠 (察) 神而同, 〔察同〕而欽 (歆), 戠 (察) 欽 (歆) 而困, 戠 (察) 困而退 (復) 。氏 (是) 古 (故) 陳為新, 人死退 (復) 為人, 水退 (復) 於天。凸 (凡) 百勿 (物) 不死女 (如) 月。出惻 (則) 或 (又) 内

(入), 冬 (終) 則或 (又) 詢 (始), 至則或 (又) 反。戡 (察) 此言, 记 (起) 於馼 (一) 耑 (端)。

It has been said: One knows by understanding the reality of things, becomes divine by discerning knowledge, becomes the same by discerning divineness, becomes reserved by discerning sameness, becomes distressed by discerning what has been reserved, and starts over again after discerning distress. Thus the old is new, people die and go back to being people, and water returns to Heaven. As a general rule the hundred things do not die, like the moon, which comes out and goes back in, terminates and starts again, arrives and returns. Examine this teaching, and one can rise up from a single strand.

The passage begins by setting forth a sequence, from *qing* 情—literally, what lies at the core of a thing, matter, or situation—to *zhi* 知 ("knowledge"), *shen* 神 ("divineness"), *tong* 同 ("sameness"), *lian* 歛 (歛) , *kun* 困 ("distress"), and back to the beginning of the sequence, as if in a cycle, or to borrow the passage's own metaphor, like the waxing and waning of the moon. The only item that requires an explanation is *lian*, which I translate as the noun "reserve." Such a reading links *tong* ("sameness") before it to *kun* ("distress") after it. The former has the sense that an unrivalled insight into the genuine reality of things enables one to merge and become one with them. Recall the ideal of "the basic rules of self-preservation" as redefined by Laozi in "Gengsang Chu" of the *Zhuangzi*: 與物委蛇, 而同其波 "To traipse and trail about with other things, to ride along with them on the same wave," or such expressions as "mysterious virtue" (*xuande*) and "mysterious mirror" (*xuanlan*) from chapter 10 of the *Laozi*; the word "mysterious" implies a kind of general resemblance where all differences and distinctions are obscured.[24] As for *kun* ("distress"), this signals a turn, the beginning of decline in life's journey, and it ultimately concludes with death and the beginning of a new life cycle.

Sandwiched between these two terms, *lian* denotes a transition from flourish to decline, from life to death. Thus, rather than reading it with a meaning close to either *tong* ("sameness") or *kun* ("distress"), as has been proposed by previous scholars, I would suggest that *lian* has the meaning of "to gather" or "to accumulate," on the one hand, and "to reduce," on the other. This latter is in the sense that things have been brought together and collected in one place, thus becoming inaccessible elsewhere. This dual meaning is captured in a text from the *New Documents* (Xinshu) called

"Methods of the Way" (Daoshu 道術), which offers the following definition: 廣較自歛謂之儉，反儉為侈 "To measure broadly and *lian* ['accumulate'] for one's own purpose is called *jian* ['frugal']; the opposite of frugal is extravagant."[25] It is possible for *lian* and *jian* 儉 to gloss each other, not only because they share the same phonetic component and are thus homophonous or nearly so in the language of ancient China but also because the two meanings are related: being frugal is what enables one to accumulate, and to accumulate in one turn is to be frugal in another. Compare chapter 67 of the *Laozi*, where *jian*—one of the "three treasures" (*sanbao* 三寶) according to this text—is defined as the following: 儉故能廣 "Being frugal one could afford to be magnanimous." That is to say, the ruler's frugality only limits his personal spending; but from the perspective of the people, this frugality is actually quite beneficial, and it is what ultimately makes the ruler appear generous or magnanimous, the opposite of what we would usually expect from one's being frugal. Notice how in both of these passages, *guang* 廣 corresponds to *tong* ("sameness") from "All Things Flow into Form." As both "accumulation" and "frugality," *lian/jian* provides a transition from "sameness" to "distress" and allows us to make sense of the passage from "All Things Flow into Form" as a whole. By being the same as others, I am able to amass all the energy generated from this sameness ("one becomes reserved by discerning sameness"). However, such amassing or "reservation" also implies a kind of contraction, and this is what ultimately leads to the distress in the phrase that follows ("one becomes distressed by discerning what has been reserved").

For one more attestation of the dual meanings of *lian* as both "to accumulate" and "to be frugal," consider the quotation from chapter 67 of the *Laozi* in the *Han Feizi*. This is a text called "Commentaries on Laozi's Teachings" (Jie Lao 解老):

周公曰：「冬日之閉凍也不固，則春夏之長草木也不茂。」天地不能常侈常費，而況於人乎？故萬物必有盛衰，萬事必有弛張，國家必有文武，官治必有賞罰。是以智士儉用其財則家富，聖人愛寶其神則精盛，人君重戰其卒則民眾，民眾則國廣。是以舉之曰：「儉，故能廣。」[27]

The Duke of Zhou said: "If it does not freeze hard in winter days, grass and trees will not flourish in spring and summer." Even heaven and earth cannot always be extravagant and lavish, how much less can mankind be so? Therefore, the myriad things prosper and decline, the myriad affairs must become taut and slack, the state must have civil and military institutions, and government must have reward and punishment. For this reason, if wise men are frugal with their wealth, their families will become rich; if the sage treasures his spirit, his essential energy will become abundant; and if the ruler does not take lightly employing his soldiers for battles, his subjects will become numerous. If the subjects are numerous, the state will become magnanimous. From all these facts there can be inferred the saying: "Being frugal one could afford to be magnanimous."

It is by being frugal that one accumulates wealth, just as the maintenance of one's spirit enables the essential energy to flourish, or the ruler's care for his people attracts them to gather around him. But scarcity is a possibility never far from sight. This is the cycle of flourish and decline that the passage describes as the following: 故萬物必有盛衰, 萬事必有弛張 "Therefore, the myriad things prosper and decline, the myriad affairs must become taut and slack." Notice how this cyclical motion corresponds to "All Things Flow into Form," with its discussion of water returning to Heaven, of the moon's waxing and waning, and most importantly, of humans dying and returning to being humans, a topic that I will turn to presently. For "All Things Flow into Form," understanding this cycle is to grasp the principle denoted by *yiduan* 一端 ("a single strand") at the very end of the discussion. As is consistent with the rest of the second part of "All Things Flow into Form," such principle enables one to respond to the myriad things and their endless variations.

If, with this understanding, we now go back to the first part of "All Things Flow into Form," then we might have a different reading of a discussion about the numinousness of ghosts. This passage begins with the question: 吾既長而又老, 孰為薦奉? 鬼生於人, 奚故神明 "When I have grown frail and old, who will serve me? If ghosts are born from people, for what reason are they divinely intelligent?" That is, how did ghosts become superhuman if they had once been human like us? This is followed by a series of questions about how ghosts should be served, and it ends with three consecutive questions that encapsulate the discussion: 天之明奚得? 鬼之神奚食? 先王之智奚備 "In what way is Heaven's brilliance attained? In what way are ghosts fed, numinous as they are? By what means was the wisdom of the kings of old so complete?" Note that the juxtaposition of *ming* 明 ("brilliance") and *shen* ("divineness") corresponds to *shenming* 神明 ("divine intelligence") from the beginning of the passage. As for the question about the ancient sages, this could be understood in a general sense, but in the context of the preceding two questions, it could also take on a more specific meaning in connection with ghosts: how were the ancient sages so wise that they knew to do the right thing in dealing with ghosts?

This is the passage in full (slips 5–8):

虗 (吾) 既長而或 (又) 老, 簹 (孰) 為𢆶 (薦) 奉? 視 (鬼) 生於人, 系 (奚) 古 (故) 神㮴 (明)? 視 (鬼) 生於人, 系 (奚) 古 (故) 神㮴 (明)? 骨= (骨肉) 之既㱙 (靡), 丌 (其) 智 (智) 愈暲 (彰), 丌 (其) 夬 (訣) 系 (奚) 䢃 (適), 簹 (孰) 䎽 (知) 丌 (其) 疆 (彊)? 視 (鬼) 生於人, 虗 (吾) 系 (奚) 古 (故) 事之? 骨= (骨肉) 之既㱙 (靡), 身豊 (體) 不見, 虗 (吾) 系 (奚) 自飤 (食) 之? 丌 (其) 㣟 (來) 亡 (無) 尻 (度), 虗 (吾) 系 (奚) 㣄 (待) 之窐 (窟)? 祭員〈異〉(祀) 系 (奚) 逐, 虗 (吾) 女 (如) 之可 (何) 思 (使) 豰 (飽)? 川 (順) 天之道, 虗 (吾) 系 (奚) 㠯 (以) 為頁 (首)? 虗 (吾) 欲㝵 (得) 百眚 (姓) 之和, 虗 (吾) 系 (奚) 事之歔 (重)? 天之㮴 (明) 系 (奚) 㝵 (得)? 視 (鬼) 之神系 (奚) 飤 (食)? 先王之 䎽 (智) 系 (奚) 備?

When I have grown frail and old, who will serve me? If ghosts are born from people, for what reason are they divinely intelligent? What makes it that, when flesh and bones have disintegrated, their wisdom is even more manifest? What place do they go upon bidding farewell? Who knows their domain? Ghosts are born from people. What requires me to serve them? When flesh and bones have disintegrated, their bodies no longer visible, why do I feed them? Their coming and going have no regularity, how do I wait for them by the grave? How do sacrifices reach them? What do I do to satiate them? In complying with the Way of Heaven, what do I make my first priority? If I want to have harmony among the people, on which affairs do I place the greatest weight? In what way is Heaven's brilliance attained? In what way are ghosts fed, numinous as they are? By what means was the wisdom of the kings of old so complete?

Comparing this with the aforementioned passage from "All Things Flow into Form," it seems to me that the connection between the two is clear. The first part of the text asks about ghosts, particularly what makes them superhuman, and the second states that life and death are part of a cycle: "People die and go back to being people." Notice how the *shen* ("divineness") that is at the heart of the questions posed in the first part of the text now becomes only one stage in the sequence: "One becomes divine by discerning knowledge, becomes the same by discerning divineness," and so forth. This accepts that ghosts have a superhuman capacity but subsumes it under a higher, broader principle, that is, the notion of Oneness.

For "All Things Flow into Form," the significance of this connection is that the two parts of the text have an integral relation with one another: one should not be read in isolation of the other, and the discussion in the second part can be understood as a direct reply to the questions posed in the first part.[28] This connection has another implication: the discussion of "All Things Flow into Form," particularly the repeated emphasis on the notion of Oneness in the second part of the text, is directed at a target, perhaps a competing teaching. In this particular instance, it is the belief in the superhuman capacity of ghosts, one that "All Things Flow into Form" wishes to allocate to a secondary place. This is consistent with several discussions with which "All Things Flow into Form" shares the same rhetorical formula, as mentioned before; they are "Gengsang Chu" of the *Zhuangzi* and the two *Guanzi* texts.

Of course, the broader context of all this is what Qian Mu 錢穆 (1895–1990) refers to in his classic article, "The Cosmologies of the Commentaries of the *Book of Changes* and the *Records of the Rites*" (Yizhuan yu Xiao Dai liji zhong zhi yuzhou lun 易傳與小戴禮記中之宇宙論), as the effort by Confucian thought toward the late Warring States period to incorporate cosmology into its tradition.[29] As pointed out by Qian Mu, this body of discourse differs from its counterparts, the earlier discussions of cosmology in Daoist works like the *Zhuangzi*, in that it presents an ethical vision of the cosmos, emphasizing such attributes as constancy (*heng* 恆), distinctness (*chengming* 誠明), and generation and completion (*shengcheng huayu* 生成化育). Such discourse also signals an attempt to move away from an earlier, more primordial credence that is the belief in the supernatural. While all of these characterizations apply to "All Things Flow into Form," the last item is probably the one most pertinent to our discussion in this chapter. In rejecting divination, physiological exercises, offerings to the spirits, and whatnot, "All Things Flow into Form" is shifting its attention to the ethical, universalizing, and distinct principle that is Oneness.

This being said, "All Things Flow into Form" also helps us revise Qian Mu's sweeping narrative in a major way: it can move the developments that

Qian Mu speaks of to an earlier date. If, in the past, Qian Mu and other scholars focused on the evolution of such notions as yin and yang, Heaven and Earth, the four seasons, and even the five agents, they did not pay sufficient attention to Oneness. With the discovery of "All Things Flow into Form" (and what I suggest here applies to the Guodian text "Grand One Gives Birth to Water" as well), we can begin to understand the discussion of Oneness as being part of this development.[30]

Concluding Remarks

This study began as an effort to resolve some of the thorniest problems in the reading of "All Things Flow into Form." For *shao che* 少啟, we saw how it is possible to read the expression as *zhao che* 朝徹 ("arriving at dawn"), and in so doing, draw on the "Great and Venerable Teacher" of the *Zhuangzi* and the much more elaborate account there about a transformative experience that takes place during the night. This opened the door for us to consider various accounts in the transmitted literary record: whether it is racing with one's own shadow, standing over an abyss, or traveling night and day to seek the advice of a legendary sage, the common theme is the aloneness of a person, with no one to watch over him except himself, and with only his conscience to answer to.

For a second expression, *shao cheng* 佥城, the connection that I wished to establish is with *xiao cheng* 削成 ("paring down what is completed") from the Guodian manuscript "Grand One Gives Birth to Water." A comparison reveals two features about "All Things Flow into Form": in terms of content, the emphasis on the notion of Oneness; in terms of form, a bifurcated structure where the first part raises a series of questions about the origin of things and the second part provides the answer. In the course of my analysis, I covered various topics ranging from a spirit journey to nonaction, from the multiple constituents of the mind to the rejection of superstition. There is one final topic that requires further discussion. This is the relation between "All Things Flow into Form" and the realist position represented by Han Feizi and Shang Yang.

As shown in my analysis in chapters 2 and 3, there is a direct correlation between these two positions. One is about the ethics of the ruler. The other is about the accountability of the subjects. Though the dates of the sources suggest that the first position is generally earlier than the second, I believe the other way around is probably closer to the truth. If Han Feizi and Shang Yang themselves lived in the third century BCE, there must have been other figures hailing from earlier times who held similar views, and it was these precursors of the legalist tradition that "All Things Flowed into Form" reacted against. Thus, in this newly discovered manuscript from the Shanghai Museum, what we have is a snapshot of a perennial tug of war.

For the interest in the situation of one's being alone, whether it is discussed in terms of *yexing* ("walking in the night"), *shen qi du* ("being watchful over oneself when alone"), or *cheng* ("sincerity"), we can make a similar observation. Perhaps such an interest went back as early as the ancient conception of the ruler as a kind of channel between the humans and a higher power, a role that is best exemplified in the ruler's self-reference, "I the lone man" (*yu yiren* 余一人), an evocative expression attested in the earliest written records, both transmitted and excavated.[1] If we find traces of these discussions in "All Things Flow into Form," it is because this manuscript made an effort to draw from an inherited discourse that had deep roots in the past. What is significant, of course, is that "All Things Flow into Form" took a turn toward what is internal to oneself.

Consider the formulation of "the heart of hearts." As I pointed out in chapter 3, such an expression was by no means the invention of "All Things Flow into Form," and it can be traced to earlier discussions centered on such maxims as "Return to the observance of the rites through overcoming oneself" (*ke ji fu li*), "He who overcomes himself is strong" (*zi sheng zhi wei qiang*), or "Overcome oneself and set the standard" (*zi sheng li zhong*). All of them recognize the struggle that takes place within oneself, but if they are somewhat vague on the outcome—after one has overcome oneself, what follows?—it is "All Things Flow into Form" and the texts closely related to it that turn the focus to the mind: some parts of it should be cast off and some parts maintained and cultivated. From here it is possible to discuss what is inherent to the mind and what is not, a next step that is easy to take, or perhaps simply an alternative approach that someone with a slightly different emphasis might adopt. We may consider the example of Xunzi. As I showed in chapter 4, even though Xunzi is critical of the formulation of "the heart of hearts," he still shares with it the same concern over the unity of the mind. Thus, there are interesting differences to explore among this small group of thinkers, even though the differences may seem inconsequential when viewed from a broader perspective. Such is the disinterested approach adopted by figures like Han Feizi and Shang Yang, who have little concern for the workings of the mind apart from how they may be exploited for the benefit of the ruler.

In the end, the significance of "All Things Flow into Form" lies in its advocacy of a vision that can be extended to every person alike, not just an instrument of control and dominance. If we are talking about the mind that everyone has, then the ruler is held to the same standard as the common person. What he imposes onto others will come back to himself. Ultimately, this is what I think makes "All Things Flow into Form" and the whole body of discourse that it represents so relevant, then as now.

For a text that is so concerned with the question of origins, one wants to know where "All Things Flow into Form" comes from. This is a question that, like the text itself, can be asked an infinite number of times. Whatever the answer, one can always turn it into yet another question: but where does this answer originate? And so on. Thus, the following is not intended to provide some kind of ultimatim, as if to fix an origin and clear away all doubts once and for all; it is simply considering some sources that I believe are relevant to "All Things Flow into Form." Many of these have been discussed by previous scholars in connection with "Heavenly Questions" (Tianwen 天問), a poem from the same poetry anthology, *The Songs of the South*, as "Far-off Journey" (Yuanyou), though I find this work so exceptional that it seems more interesting to consider not the poem itself but the background that it might have shared with "All Things Flow into Form."[2]

The first of these related sources is the opening passage of a text in the *Zhuangzi* called "The Turning of Heaven" (Tianyun 天運):

天其運乎？地其處乎？日月其爭於所乎？孰主張是？孰維綱是？孰居无事推而行是？意者其有機緘而不得已邪？意者其運轉而不能自止邪？雲者為雨乎？雨者為雲乎？孰隆施是？孰居无事淫樂而勸是？風起北方，一西一東，有上彷徨，孰噓吸是？孰居无事而披拂是？敢問何故。

巫咸祒曰：「來！吾語女。天有六極五常，帝王順之則治，逆之則凶。九洛之事，治成德備，監照下土，天下載之，此謂上皇。」[3]

Does Heaven turn? Does the earth sit still? Do sun and moon compete for a place to shine? Who masterminds all this? Who pulls the strings? Who, resting inactive himself, gives the push that makes it go this way? I wonder, is there some mechanism that works[4] it and won't let it stop? I wonder if it just rolls and turns and can't bring itself to a halt? Do the clouds make the rain, or does the rain make the clouds? Who puffs them up, who showers them down like this? Who, resting inactive himself, stirs up all this lascivious joy? The winds rise in the north, blowing now west, now east, whirling up to wander on high. Whose breaths and exhalations are they? Who, resting inactive himself, huffs and puffs them about like this? I dare ask the reason why.

Shaman Xian Zhao said, "Come—I will tell you. Heaven has the six directions and the five constants. When emperors and kings go along with these, there is good order; when they move contrary to these, there is disaster. With the instructions of the Nine Luo,[5] order can be made to reign and virtue completed. The ruler will shine mirror-like over the earth below, and the world will bear him up. He may be called an August One on High."

This passage consists of two parts: the first raises a series of questions about Heaven, Earth, and the forces of nature, and this resembles the first part of "All Things Flow into Form." The second is an answer to those questions: although it does not directly identify the prime moving force behind the phenomena of nature, it suggests that such a force was heeded by the ancient sages, and one who aligns himself with it can be called the "August One on High" (Shanghuang 上皇).

The second passage is a text from the *Annals of Lü Buwei* called "Knowing the Measure" (Zhi du 知度):

人主自智而愚人，自巧而拙人，若此則愚拙者請矣，巧智者詔矣。詔多則請者愈多矣，請者愈多，且無不請也。主雖巧智，未無不知也。以未無不知，應無不請，其道固窮。為人主而數窮於其下，將何以君人乎？窮而不知其窮，其患又將反以自多，是之謂重塞。重塞[6]之主，無存國矣。故有道之主，因而不為，責而不詔，去想去意，靜虛以待，不代[7]之言，不奪之事，督名審實，官使自司，以不知為道，以奈何為寶[8]。堯曰：「若何而為及日月之所燭？」舜曰：「若何而服四荒之外？」禹曰：「若何而治青北[9]、化九陽、奇肱[10]之所際？」[11]

> When a ruler regards himself wise and others stupid, himself artful and others clumsy, the stupid and clumsy will ask directions, and the wise and artful will have to inform them. The more they have to inform, the more requests there will be for directions; and as these requests increase, there will be nothing about which the stupid and clumsy will not ask for direction. However clever and wise the ruler may be, he can never know everything. If one who does not know everything responds to every request, his Dao will assuredly meet its limitations. If a ruler meets the limitations of his techniques in dealing with his own subordinates, how then will he act as lord to others? Having met his limitations and failed to realize they are limitations increases the problems that burden him. This is what is meant by being "doubly impeded." A ruler who is doubly impeded will not keep his state. A ruler who possesses the Dao, therefore, relies on others and does not act, assigns duties but does not inform. He discards conceptualization and imagination, and awaits results in quiescence and emptiness. He does not substitute his words for theirs, nor does he usurp their tasks; but he inspects the names and examines the reality, and the officials thereby manage things themselves. He takes "not knowing" as his Dao, and "what should I do?" as his treasure.
>
> Yao asked, "How do my actions illuminate the world as do the sun and moon?" Shun asked, "How do I bring to submission those beyond the distant realms of the four quarters?" Yu asked, "How do I bring to order Qingqiu and transform the boundary areas of Jiuyang and Qigong?"

As with "The Turning of Heaven," this passage consists of two parts: one that is an exposition of a principle, and the other a series of questions for which the same principle could provide an answer. Because the series of questions appear at the end of the passage, they seem to be rhetorical in nature, but if they had appeared at the beginning of the passage, they would have resembled the questions from the *Zhuangzi* and indeed "All Things Flow into Form." This is further indication that any time a question is raised, it is inevitably accompanied by an answer, even if that answer is a silent one.

The third example is the manuscript from the Han tomb at Mawangdui, "Ten Questions" (Shiwen). Besides the dialogue cited in chapter 1, there is another that resembles "All Things Flow into Form" rather closely. This is the fourth of the ten dialogues, an exchange between the Yellow Thearch

(Huangdi 黃帝) and the sage Rong Cheng 容成, who is evidently even more distinguished than him (slips 23–29, 52–59):

> 黃帝問於容成曰:「民始蒲 (敷) 淳溜 (流) 刑 (形), 何得而生? 溜 (流) 刑 (形) 成體 (體), 何失而死? 何與 (猶) 之人也, 有惡有好, 有夭有壽? 欲聞民氣贏屈施 (弛) 張之故。」¹²

> The Yellow Thearch asked Rong Cheng: "When people first dispense the purity and flow into form, how do they get to be born? Having flown into form and completed the body, how do they lose it and die? How is it that all are people alike, yet some are foul while others are fair, some die young while others are long-lived? I wish to hear the reason why people's energy thrives or shrinks, why it slackens or expands."

The dialogue continues with a detailed discussion of *qi*, a part of which I have already alluded to in chapter 1 when discussing the physiological basis for the process of self-cultivation that takes place at night. Interestingly, the dialogue ends with Rong Cheng making a reference to Wu Cheng Zhao 巫成柖, a variant of Wu Xian Zhao 巫咸柖 that we saw in "The Turning of the Heaven" from the *Zhuangzi*.¹³ Unfortunately, the many lacuna in this part of the manuscript prevents us from knowing exactly what it says.

There is one more example to be mentioned, also the most important, but perhaps we can already see from the ones cited so far that all of them are a combination of questions and answers. To be sure, there are variations: "The Turning of Heaven" has the questions preceding the answers, and for "Knowing the Measure" it is the opposite. "Ten Questions" is also considerably longer than the other two texts. But the combination is what it is, and I would suggest seeing these texts as three examples of the same format. Such a format can be a vehicle for transmitting different kinds of information and ideology. For "Knowing the Measure" to suggest that the ruler should simply act according to the way things are and not impose his limited understanding on the world, it is hinting at the teaching of "Following" (*Yinxun* 因循) often associated with Shenzi 慎子 (fourth century BCE). As for "Ten Questions," while some parts of the fourth dialogue are useful for understanding the conception of a journey in the night, this discussion of *qi* must be placed in the overall context of the topic that pervades the rest of this dialogue, or the Art of the Bedchamber. The closest match with "All Things Flow into Form" in terms of content is "The

Turning of Heaven." Indeed, by suggesting that the prime moving force behind natural phenomena nature was grasped by the ancient sages, this text from the *Zhuangzi* attempts to pinpoint a principle that is otherwise elusive. This could also be said to be the import of "All Things Flow into Form."

As shown in the last section before these concluding remarks, "All Things Flow into Form" has a bifurcated structure not unlike the three texts cited here: a first part that asks the questions and a second part that identifies Oneness as the answer to those questions. Considered together, we can see that it is not necessary to distinguish the two parts, as if they were separated by some kind of gap or came from two different hands. Instead, both question and answer go together and cannot exist independent of one another. In terms of the structure of "All Things Flow into Form," the most important parallel is perhaps "Grand One Gives Birth to Water." I have already mentioned that this text contains the expression *xiao cheng* ("paring down what is completed"), which alerts us to identifying the same expression in "All Things Flow into Form." Even more significantly, this text from Guodian is comparable to "All Things Flow into Form" in that it is also divided into two parts. One asks for the name of the principle behind Heaven, Earth, and the myriad things; if it is not the Way (Dao) as commonly assumed, then what is it? The other goes ahead and identifies "Grand One" (Taiyi) as this principle. Given that the dates for both of these texts are somewhat indeterminate, one must resort to the contents to decide which is earlier. One indication is that whereas "Grand One Gives Birth to Water" makes a formal request to know about the principle underlying all things, or the principle of Oneness, "All Things Flow into Form" simply implies this fact. It would have been odd if "Grand One Gives Birth to Water" was the later of the two; the request to know about Grand One would have been completely gratuitous. In addition, there are several more indirect reasons why I think "Grand One Gives Birth to Water" precedes "All Things Flow into Form."

The first is that the "Grand One Gives Birth to Water" has a relationship with "All Things Flow into Form" that is comparable to that between another pair of newly excavated texts, "Five Conducts" (Wuxing) and its commentary. As it is well known, the former hails from the same corpus as "Grand One Gives Birth to Water," and the latter is attested only in the copy of "Five Conducts" found in the Han tomb at Mawangdui. While "Five Conducts" itself speaks repeatedly of the principle of Oneness, much like "Grand One Gives Birth to Water," it is only in the commentary that the discussion of Oneness also refers to "a flowing body" (*liu ti* 流體), a term that is basically the same as the "flowing form" (*liu xing* 流形) which headlines "All Things Flow into Form."[14] Given the likelihood of a time gap between "Five Conducts" and its commentary, this evidence is consistent with the suggestion that "Grand One Gives Birth to Water" precedes "All Things Flow into Form."

For another indication of the relatively late date of "All Things Flow into Form," we may turn to the text from the *Guanzi* called "Inner Workings" (Neiye), cited in chapter 5. The passage under consideration begins with the discussion that "the Way fills the whole world" (*Dao man tianxia* 道滿天下). This is followed by the suggestion that it can be "explained with one saying" (*yiyan zhi jie* 一言之解). The text poses a rhetorical question: "What do we mean by understanding it?" (*he wei jie zhi* 何謂解之). And the answer: "This lies in the mind's being at ease" (*zai yu xin an* 在於心安). The text goes on to give its formulation of "the heart of hearts."[15] Here we find a sequence from the Way to the principle of Oneness and ultimately to the mind. The logic is clear: by coming to terms with one's mind and grasping the principle of Oneness, one finds the Way. Comparing this with "All Things Flow into Form," it is noteworthy that this newly discovered text also speaks of the mind, Oneness, and the Way (even though this last item has a relatively marginal place, perhaps due to all the emphasis on Oneness). By contrast, "Grand One Gives Birth to Water" does not refer to the mind at all. This is perhaps also an indication of the relative dates of "Grand One Gives Birth to Water" and "All Things Flow into Form": the former was composed at a time when the discussion of the mind was not yet prevalent, and it was only in the latter that this interest was reflected.[16]

Finally, regarding the formulation of "the heart of hearts," it seems to me that we may gain a further insight by setting this against two opposing notions in ancient intellectual discourse. The first is *zhong* 中 ("inner core"), most famously seen in "Doctrine of the Mean" (Zhongyong), but in various other ancient texts as well.[17] The second is *chong* 沖 ("emptiness"), seen in several passages in the *Laozi* (especially chapter 45) and the *Zhuangzi*.[18] The two words may be related in the sense that they represent two different conceptions of the ideal for one's inner capacity. For "Doctrine of the Mean" and many ancient sources, what is internal to oneself is real and substantial, whether it is virtue taking form within oneself, a fundamental goodness deeply rooted in oneself, or a state of equilibrium attained by oneself. By contrast, for the *Laozi* and *Zhuangzi*, the ideal is emptiness, or the rejection of any conscious activity stemming from oneself. The formulation of "the heart of hearts," when compared with these two notions, seems to be an attempt to reconcile them. While recognizing that part of the mind can be discarded, it also identifies a core that must be preserved. Once again, because both *zhong* and *chong* can be found in the Guodian texts, this is perhaps another indication that "All Things Flow into Form" is later.[19]

This study began with an analysis of "The Great and Venerable Teacher" of the *Zhuangzi*. As we approach the end, it is perhaps fitting to return to the same work and consider the following passage from "Ze Yang" 則陽. This is a passage familiar to readers of the *Laozi*; in its discussion of the Way, its vastness, its ineffability, and the futility of trying to understand it according to conventional thinking, "Ze Yang" resembles this classic of five thousand characters. It is also valuable for alluding to teachings that may have been popular at one point but which are now only partially reflected in the transmitted literary record. None of these teachings has a one-to-one relation with "All Things Flow into Form," but an understanding of what they are and the kind of debate they helped to generate can help us put that newly discovered manuscript into perspective. We will see against this broader context that "All Things Flow into Form" was just one more response to a question that puzzled numerous thinkers, from the theorists behind the teachings of *mo wei* 莫為 ("nothing does it") and *huo shi* 或使 ("something makes it like this") to the author of "Ze Yang." In particular, this is the question about a prime moving force of the world.

This passage is the last to appear in "Ze Yang." It begins with Shaozhi 少知 ("Little Understanding") posing a question to Taigong Tiao 太公調 ("Great Impartial Accord"):

少知問於太公調曰:「何謂丘里之言?」太公調曰:「丘里者, 合十姓百名而以為風俗也。合異以為同, 散同以為異。今指馬之百體而不得馬, 而馬係於前者, 立其百體而謂之馬也。是故丘山積卑而為高, 江河合水而為大, 大人合并而為公。是以自外入者, 有主而不執; 由中出者, 有正而不距。四時殊氣, 天不賜, 故歲成; 五官殊職, 君不私, 故國治; 文武殊能[20], 大人不賜, 故德備; 萬物殊理, 道不私, 故无名。无名故无為, 无為而无不為。時有終始, 世有變化。禍福淳淳, 至有所拂者而有所宜; 自殉殊面, 有所正者有所差。比于大澤, 百材皆度; 觀乎大山, 木石同壇。此之謂丘里之言。」

Little Understanding asked Great Impartial Accord, "What is meant by the term 'community words'?" Great Impartial Accord said, "'Community words' refers to the combining of ten surnames and a hundred given names and regarding this as the custom. Differences are combined into a sameness; sameness are broken into differences. Now we may point to each of the hundred parts of a horse's body and never come up with a 'horse'—yet here is the horse, tethered right before our eyes. So we take the hundred parts and set up the term 'horse.' Thus it is that hills and mountains pile up one little layer on another to reach loftiness; the Yangzi and the Yellow River combine stream after stream to achieve magnitude; and the Great Man combines and brings together things to attain generality. Therefore, things that enter the mind from the outside make one determined, but not stubborn; and things that come forth from the mind sets a standard, but does not distance oneself from others. The four seasons each differ in breath, but Heaven does not bestow special favors, and therefore the year comes to completion. The five government bureaus differ in function, but the ruler shows no partiality among them, and therefore the state is well ordered. In both civil and military affairs, the Great Man does not bestow special favors, and therefore his virtue is complete. The ten thousand things differ in principle, but the Way shows no partiality among them, and therefore it is nameless. Being nameless, it is without action; without action, yet there is nothing it does not do. The seasons have their end and beginning, the ages their changes and transformations. Bad fortunes and good, tripping and tumbling, come now with what repels you, now with what you welcome. What each person pursues is different, now you judge things to be upright, now you judge them to be warped. But if you could only be like the great swamp, which finds accommodation for a hundred different timbers, or take your model from the great mountain, whose trees and rocks share a common ground! This is what is meant by the term 'community words.'"

The passage begins by defining what it calls "community words" (*qiuli zhi yan* 丘里之言), where the said community is a social unit that consists of a small number of residents and is parallel to the Way: just as a community is a collection of households, the Way is made up of the myriad things, and just as a community has customs, an identity (literally *tong*, or "sameness") that distinguishes it from other communities, the Way can be thought of as the principle behind the cyclical motions of the myriad things. The point is to move beyond the limited perspective of oneself and adopt a broader view, whether this is from the perspective of a community or the much more general Way.

In the following section, the discussion makes a point about the ineffability of the Way that resembles the *Laozi*, in both the opening chapter and chapter 25. Responding to Little Understanding's question about a name for the Way, Great Impartial Accord concedes the epithet but adds that this is done merely out of convenience. The fact is that the Way or the principle identified by it cannot be named. Any attempt to do so would be diminishing it; the distance between name and reality is like that between the cries of animals and the analytical language employed by philosophers:

少知曰：「然則謂之道，足乎？」太公調曰：「不然。今計物之數，不止於萬，而期曰萬物者，以數之多者號而讀之也。是故天地者，形之大者也；陰陽者，氣之大者也。道者為之公，因其大以號而讀之則可也。已有之矣，乃將得比哉，則若以斯辯譬猶狗馬，其不及遠矣。」

Little Understanding said, "Well, then, if we call it the Way, will that be sufficient?" "Oh, no," said Great Impartial Accord. "If we calculate the number of things that exist, the count certainly does not stop at ten thousand. Yet we set a limit and speak of the 'ten thousand things'—because we select a number that is large and agree to apply it to them. In the same way, heaven and earth are forms which are large, the yin and yang are breaths which are large, and the Way is the generality that embraces them. If from the point of view of largeness we agree to give it this name, then there is no objection. But if, having established this name, we go on to compare it to other things, then it will be like using clever words to debate with dogs and horses—the distance between them is impossibly far."

The discussion continues by pointing out the vastness and complexity of things. Just as it makes no sense to name the Way, it is a waste of time to try to pinpoint a single origin from which things emerged. The operations of the world take place cyclically, constantly, and endlessly. Rather than trying to apply one's words and understanding to this ultimate mystery, it is better to simply acknowledge one's limitation and admire the Way for what it is:

少知曰：「四方之內，六合之裏，萬物之所生惡起？」太公調曰：「陰陽相照、相蓋、相治，四時相代、相生、相殺，欲惡去就於是橋起，雌雄片合於是庸有。安危相易，禍福相生，緩急相摩，聚散以成。此名實之可紀，精之可志也。隨序之相理，橋運之相使，窮則反，終則始，此物之所有。言之所盡，知之所至，極物而已。觀道之人，不隨其所廢，不原其所起，此議之所止。」

Little Understanding said, "Here within the four directions and the six realms, where do the ten thousand things spring from when they come into being?" Great Impartial Accord said, "The yin and yang shine on each other, maim each other, heal each other; the four seasons succeed each other, give birth to each other, slaughter each other. Desire and hatred, rejection and acceptance thereupon rise up in succession; the pairing of halves between male and female thereupon becomes a regular occurrence. Security and danger trade places with each other, bad and good fortune give birth to each other, tense times and relaxed ones buffet one another, gathering-together and scattering bring it all to completion. These names and realities can be recorded, their details and minute parts can be noted. The principle of following one another in orderly succession, the property of moving in alternation, turning back when they have reached the limit, beginning again when they have ended—these are inherent in things. But that which words can adequately describe, that which understanding can reach to, extends only as far as the level of 'things,' no farther. The man who looks to the Way does not try to track down what has disappeared, does not try to trace the source of what springs up. This is the point at which debate comes to a stop."

In the last part of this passage, the discussion refers to two teachings: *mo wei* ("nothing does it") and *huo shi* ("something makes it like this"), as advocated by Jizhen 季真 and Jiezi 接子, respectively.[21] These two teachings offer contrasting perspectives to the common question about a prime driving force. *Mo wei* says there is nothing, that things are the way they are for no particular reason. *Huo shi*, by contrast, posits that there is something. Who is right? Little Understanding asks. As Great Impartial Accord explains, neither of these teachings comes at the question in the right way. Though one can be said to be "substantial" (*shi* 實) and the other "empty" (*xu* 虛), they are both stuck at the level of things. Thus: 或使則實, 莫為則虛; 有名有實, 是物之居; 无名无實, 在物之虛 "If 'something makes it like this,' then it is substantial; if 'nothing does it,' then it is empty. While there are names and realities, you are in the presence of things. When there are no names and realities, you exist in the absence of things." As much as they try to describe and speculate about this prime driving force, they only remove themselves farther away from the truth: 可言可意, 言而愈疏 "You can talk about it, you can think about it; but the more you talk about it, the farther away you get from it." Instead, we should look beyond the distinction drawn by these teachings and recognize the broader underlying principle, which is neither this nor that, neither "being" (*you* 有) nor "nonbeing" (*wu* 无), neither words nor silence. Such a principle can be called "Principle" (*li* 理), the Way, or "the Great Method" (*defang* 大方), but these terms are simply given for the sake of convenience. The discussion ends on this point, calling for the termination of all such discussions:

少知曰:「季真之莫為, 接子之或使, 二家之議, 孰正於其情, 孰偏於其理?」太公調曰:「雞鳴狗吠, 是人之所知; 雖有大知, 不能以言讀其所自化, 又不能以意測[22]其所將為。斯而析之, 精至於无倫, 大至於不可圍, 或之使, 莫之為, 未免於物而終以為過。或使則實, 莫為則虛。有名有實, 是物之居; 无名无實, 在物之虛。可言可意, 言而愈疏。未生不可忌, 已死不可阻。死生非遠也, 理不可覩。或之使, 莫之為, 疑之所假。吾觀之本, 其往无窮; 吾求之末, 其來无止。无窮无止, 言之无也, 與物同理; 或使莫為, 言之本也, 與物終始。道不可有, 有不可無, 道之為名, 所假而行。或使莫為, 在物一曲, 夫胡為於大方? 言而足, 則終日言而盡道; 言而不足, 則終日言而盡物。道物之極, 言默不足以載; 非言非默, 議有所極。」[23]

Little Understanding said, "Jizhen's contention that 'nothing does it' and Jiezi's contention that 'something makes it like this'—of the views of these two schools, which correctly describes the truth of the matter and which is one-sided in its understanding of principles?" Great Impartial Accord said, "Chickens squawk, dogs bark—this is something men understand. But no matter how great their understanding, they cannot explain in words how the chicken and the dog have come to be what they are, nor can they imagine in their minds what they will become in the future. You may pick apart and analyze till you have reached what is so minute that it is without form, what is so large that it cannot be encompassed. But whether you say that 'nothing does it' or that 'something makes it like this,' you have not yet escaped from the realm of 'things,' and so in the end you fall into error. If 'something makes it like this,' then it is substantial; if 'nothing does it,' then it is empty. While there are names and realities, you are in the presence of things. When there are no names and realities, you exist in the absence of things. You can talk about it, you can think about it; but the more you talk about it, the farther away you get from it. Before they are born, things cannot decline to be born; already dead, they cannot refuse to go. Death and life are not far apart, though the principle that underlies them cannot be seen. 'Nothing does it,' 'something makes it like this'—these are speculations born out of doubt. I look for the roots of the past, but they extend back and back without end. I search for the termination of the future, but it never stops coming at me. Without end, without stop, it is the absence of words, which shares the same principle with things themselves. But 'nothing does it,' 'something makes it like this'—these are the commencement of words and they begin and end along with things. The Way cannot be thought of as being, nor can it be thought of as nonbeing. In calling it the Way we are only adopting a temporary expedient. 'Nothing does it,' 'something makes it like this'—these occupy a mere corner of the realm of things. What connection could they have with the Great Method? If words are sufficient, then you can talk all day long and exhaust the Way. If they are not, then you exhaust merely things by the end of the day. The perfection of the Way and things—neither words nor silence are enough for expressing it. Not to talk, not to be silent—this is the highest form of debate."

Read from beginning to end, one might come away from the passage impressed by the elegance of its presentation, even persuaded by its arguments, but stepping away for a moment, we might try to imagine this text as a response to a question, an attempt to offer a different solution than those teachings that it is so critical of. This, as I mentioned previously, is the question of a prime driving force. Whereas *mo wei* suggests that there is none, *huo shi* suggests that there is. The position of this passage is that such a discussion leads nowhere and we should simply acknowledge the limitation of our understanding. The Way as it might be called is beyond our comprehension.

It is against this background that I believe we can read "All Things Flow into Form." After all, what is the purpose of the questions that open this newly discovered manuscript if not to ask about a prime driving force? "All things flow into form; what brings them to completion? Flowing forms complete the body; what makes them never die?" So it goes. Even though "Ze Yang" does not mention "All Things Flow into Form" or the notion of Oneness so central to it, one can see how they were also part of the same debate. Like *huo shi*, the notion of Oneness points to something, though the broadness of this notion also makes the identification somewhat empty. Perhaps it was due to the frustration with this kind of ambiguity that "Ze Yang" presented its own position. Ultimately, Oneness has to come from the Way, and while one begets two, then three, and so on, there is little clue as to where everything began.[24]

Acknowledgments

Much of the research and writing for this book was done in 2017, while I was finishing *The Lost Texts of Confucius' Grandson*. Rather than a by-product of that other project, this study of a single manuscript was a mirror that I was able to hold up against my investigation into the Guodian corpus, and both books have benefitted from this back and forth. For the translation of "All Things Flow into Form" that appears at the beginning of this volume, I am grateful to Zeb Raft and Nicolas Morrow Williams for their help. Robert Campany heads a list of scholars who were kind to comment on earlier drafts, though I am perhaps too stubborn to heed all their advices. To Diao Xiaolong and Li Jing, I owe many thanks for their help on Japanese scholarship. To Christopher Pitts, for his editing of the manuscript. And to James Peltz, Aimee Harrison, and Diane Ganeles, for their overseeing of the production of the book. Roger Ames took a chance accepting this book into his series, and I join countless others before me in thanking him for his warmth, support, and open-mindedness.

Notes

Preface

1. Ma Chengyuan 馬承源, ed., *Shanghai Bowuguan cang Zhanguo Chu zhushu* 上海博物館藏戰國楚竹書 (Shanghai: Shanghai guji, 2008), vol. 7.

2. Sun Peiyang 孫沛陽, "Jiance bei huaxian chutan" 簡冊背劃線初探, *Chutu wenxian yu guwenzi yanjiu* 出土文獻與古文字研究 4 (2011): 449–62.

3. Is it ethical to study unprovenanced manuscripts such as "All Things Flow into Form"? While their study is viewed by some as abetting more tomb robberies, in the eyes of others, it is an act of salvaging. One thing is certain: more unprovenanced manuscripts are going to surface, and the debate about their study will continue. As with many things in our complex and increasingly contentious world, what one does is a matter of personal choice, even though it will inevitably be seen as taking a side.

4. The standard works in this vein are A. C. Graham, "How Much of *Chuang Tzu* Did Chuang Tzu Write?" in *Studies in Chinese Philosophy and Philosophical Literature* (Singapore: Institute of East Asian Philosophies, 1986), 283–321; and Liu Xiaogan 劉笑敢, *Zhuangzi zhexue ji qi yanbian* 莊子哲學及其演變, 2nd ed. (Zhongguo renmin daxue, 2010). The latter work was first published in 1988, and a part of it was subsequently translated into English as *Classifying the Zhuangzi Chapters* (Ann Arbor: Center for Chinese Studies, University of Michigan, 1994). In spite of the author's later efforts to respond to critics and update his findings, the main arguments—the integrity of the Inner chapters and Warring States dates for the text as a whole—have remained unchanged. These reflections can be found in the new preface to the 2010 Chinese edition and the piece "Textual Issues in the *Zhuangzi*" in Liu Xiaogan, ed., *Dao Companion to Daoist Philosophy* (New York: Springer, 2015), 129–57. For a balanced assessment, which also takes into account more recent works by David McGraw and Esther S. Klein, see Harold D. Roth, "Cognitive Attunement in the *Zhuangzi*," in Carine Defoort and Roger Ames, eds., *Having a Word with Angus Graham: On the First Quarter-Century of his Immortality* (Honolulu: University of Hawai'i Press, 2018), 75–76n34.

5. For a summary of the manuscript fragments, which have never been officially published, see Li Xueqin 李學勤, "*Zhuangzi* zapian zhujian ji qi xiangguan wenti" 《莊子·雜篇》竹簡及其相關問題, in *Li Xueqin wenji* 李學勤文集 (Shanghai: Shanghai cishu, 2005), 490–500. They are "Ze Yang" 則陽, "Giving Away a Throne" (Rang wang 讓王); "External Things" (Waiwu 外物) from a tomb in Fuyang 阜陽, Anhui; and "Robber Zhi" (Dao Zhi 盜跖) from a tomb in Zhangjiashan 張家山, Hubei. None of them is earlier than the Western Han (206 BCE–26 CE).

A Note on the Translation

1. Ma Chengyuan, ed., *Shanghai Bowuguan cang Zhanguo Chu zhushu*, vol. 7.

2. These proposals are summarized in two articles by Scott Cook, which are in effect a critical edition based on a comprehensive survey of the paleographic research, an analysis of rhyme schemes, and many of the author's own novel but widely accepted suggestions. They are merged as one in the author's essay collection in Chinese; see Gu Shikao 顧史考, "Shangbo jian 'Fan wu liu xing' shitan" 上博簡《凡物流形》試探, in *Shangbo deng Chujian Zhanguo yishu zongheng lan* 上博等楚簡戰國逸書縱橫覽 (Shanghai: Zhong Xi, 2018), 146–201. This is the basis for my reading of the "Fan wu liu xing." Other commentaries of the text can be found in *Shutsudo bunken to shinso bunka* 出土文献と秦楚文化 5 (2010): 248–82; and Yu Shaohong 俞紹宏 and Zhang Qingsong 張青松, eds., *Shanghai Bowuguan cang Zhanguo Chujian jishi* 上海博物館藏戰國楚簡集釋 (Beijing: Shehui kexue wenxian, 2019), vol. 7, 136–246. I have found the following studies useful to my understanding of the text: Asano Yūichi 浅野裕一, "Shangbo Chujian 'Fan wu liu xing' zhi zhengti jiegou" 上博楚簡《凡物流形》之整體結構, in Zhou Fengwu 周鳳五, ed., *Xian Qin wenben ji sixiang zhi xingcheng, fazhan yu zhuan* 先秦文本及思想之形成、發展與轉化 (Taipei: Taiwan daxue, 2013), 283–326; and Franklin Perkins, "Fanwu liuxing ('All Things Flow into Form') and the 'One' in the *Laozi*," *Early China* 38 (2015): 195–232. More than one article on "All Things Flow into Form" appear in each of these essay collections: Wang Zhongjiang 王中江, *Jianbo wenming yu gudai sixiang shijie* 簡帛文明與古代思想世界 (Beijing: Beijing daxue, 2011); Chen Ligui 陳麗桂, *Jin sishi nian chutu jianbo wenxian sixiang yanjiu* 近四十年出土簡帛文獻思想研究 (Taipei: Wunan, 2013); and Cao Feng 曹峰, *Jinnian chutu Huang Lao sixiang wenxian yanjiu* 近年出土黃老思想文獻研究 (Beijing: Zhongguo shehui kexue, 2015). For previous English translations, see Shirley Chan, "Oneness: Reading the 'All Things Are Flowing in Form' (Fan Wu Liu Xing)," *International Communication of Chinese Culture* 2 (2015): 285–99; and Wang Zhongjiang, *Order in Early Chinese Excavated Texts: Natural, Supernatural, and Legal Approaches* (London: Palgrave Macmillan), appendix 2.

3. "'Fan wu liu xing' kaoshi sanze" 《凡物流形》考釋三則, *Chutu wenxian* 出土文獻 14 (2019): 145–55.

Chapter 1

1. Wang Shumin 王叔岷, *Zhuangzi jiaoquan* 莊子校詮 (Taipei: Zhongyang yanjiu yuan Lishi yuyan yanjiusuo, 1988), 237–41. The translation is modified from Burton Watson, *The Complete Works of Chuang Tzu* (New York: Columbia University Press, 1968), 82–83. Another translation that is helpful is A. C. Graham, *Chuang-tzŭ: The Inner Chapters* (1981; repr., Indianapolis: Hackett, 2001), 87.

2. Hong Xingzu 洪興祖, *Chuci buzhu* 楚辭補注 (Beijing: Zhonghua, 1983). See also the more recent commentaries gathered in Jin Kaicheng 金開誠, Dong Hongli 董洪利, and Gao Luming 高路明, *Qu Yuan ji jiaozhu* 屈原集校注 (Beijing: Zhonghua, 1996). The standard translation of the *Chuci* is David Hawkes, *The Songs of the South: An Anthology of Ancient Chinese Poems by Qu Yuan and Other Poets* (Harmondsworth: Penguin, 1985). Given the iconic status of Hawkes's work, whenever our understandings differ, I will refrain from tampering with his words but explain my differences in the body of the text.

3. Hong Xingzu, *Chuci buzhu*, 299–300; Hawkes, *The Songs of the South*, 293–94. Cf. Hawkes's insightful comments about Peng Xian on 84–86.

4. Hong Xingzu, *Chuci buzhu*, 148–49; Hawkes, *The Songs of the South*, 174–75.

5. Hong Xingzu, *Chuci buzhu*, 163–64; Hawkes, *The Songs of the South*, 193–94. See also Paul W. Kroll, "On 'Far Roaming,'" *Journal of the American Oriental Society* 116, no. 4 (1996): 653–69; and "Daoist Verse and the Quest of the Divine," in John Lagerwey and Lü Pengzhi, eds., *Early Chinese Religion, Part Two: The Period of Division (220–589 AD)* (Leiden: Brill, 2010), 954–61. The classic statement about this text, which in fact juxtaposes it with the *Zhuangzi*, is Henri Maspero, "Historical Notes on the Origins and Developments of the Taoist Religion Up to the Han Period," in *Taoism and Chinese Religion* (Amherst: University of Massachusetts Press, 1981), 413–16.

6. For another instance of this, we find in "Nine Longings" (Jiusi 九思) by Wang Yi a piece called "Meeting with Reproach" (Feng you 逢尤), which contains the following line: 魂茕茕兮不遑寐，目眽眽兮寤終朝 "My soul is too restless to let me sleep at night, and I lie all the morning in staring wakefulness"; see Hong Xingzu, *Chuci buzhu*, 315–16; and Hawkes, *The Songs of the South*, 308–9. Compare this with "Nine Lamentations," particularly the piece "Saddened by Sufferings" (Youku), but a different line from the one cited earlier: 遵彼南道兮，征夫宵行 "Turning into the southward-going highway, a traveler now, he journeys through the night," which is another reference to traveling by night. Finally, in "Nine Declarations" (Jiuzhang), in the piece called "Thinking of a Fair One" (Si meiren), the aforementioned usage of *qiongqiong* is immediately preceded by the line: 命則處幽，吾將罷兮，願及白日之未暮 "It is my lot to live in darkness . . . [The day is growing dark and] draws towards its close: I must go while the bright sun has not yet reached his setting," which describes the persona's fear of an impending darkness.

7. Hong Xingzu, *Chuci buzhu*, 25–35; and Hawkes, *The Songs of the South*, 74.

8. For Fenglong 豐隆, the spirit in the clouds, see the sensible remarks by Hawkes in *The Songs of the South*, 90. Hawkes is here commenting on the appearance of this spirit in a later passage in "On Encountering Trouble." There, Fenglong plays the role of a guide in the persona's (ultimately futile) quest for another companion. As for the expression *ji chongyang* 集重陽 ("to pass through the Bright Walls"), it is not clear why Hawkes translates it the way he does. Most commentators since Wang Yi take it to refer to the aggregation of *yang* energy.

9. For "Exposition Poem on the Mighty One," see Fei Zhengang 費振剛, Qiu Zhongqian 仇仲謙, and Liu Nanping 劉南平, *Quan Hanfu jiaozhu* 全漢賦校注 (Guangzhou: Guangzhou jiaoyu, 2005), 119–25; and the translation in Burton Watson, *Records of the Grand Historian: Han Dynasty II* (Hong Kong: Chinese University Press, 1993), 298.

10. For more on the difference between "On Encountering Sorrow" and "Far-off Journey," see Kominami Ichirō 小南一郎, "Soji kōki no shosakuhin" 楚辭後期の諸作品, in *Soji to sono chūshakushatachi* 楚辭とその注釈者たち (Kyoto: Hōyū Shoten, 2003), 275; and the more general discussion in Fukunaga Mitsuji 福永光司, "Taijin fu no shisōteki keifu: Jifu no bungaku to rō sō no tetsugaku 大人賦の思想的系譜―辞賦の文学と老荘の哲学, in *Dōkyō shisōshi kenkyū* 道教思想史研究 (Tokyo: Iwanami Shoten, 1987), 265–97. Two other studies that I find useful are Sadao Takeji 竹治貞夫, "'Enyū' no seiritsu" 遠游の成立, in *Soji kenkyū* 楚辭研究 (Tokyo: Kazama Shobō, 1978), 891–920; and Yata Naoko 矢田尚子, "Soji 'Enyū' to 'Taijin fu' no tenkai yugyō" 楚辭遠游と大人賦の天界遊行, in *Soji "Risō" o yomu: higeki no chūshin Kutsu Gen no jinbutsuzō o megutte* 楚辭離騒を読む: 悲劇の忠臣・屈原の人物像をめぐって (Sendai: Tōhoku Daigaku Shuppankai, 2018), 131–62.

11. See Hawkes, *The Songs of the South*, 191–93.

12. This is from the biography of Zhuang Zhou 莊周 in *the Grand Scribe's Records*; see Takigawa Kametarō 瀧川亀太郎 and Mizusawa Toshitada 水澤利忠, *Shiji huizhu kaozheng fu jiaobu* 史記會注考證附校補 (Shanghai: Shanghai guji, 1986), 63.9–12.

13. Hawkes's translation is not impossible, but I would prefer reading the line as suggesting that one should await the Way and not try to anticipate or get before it, because the Way is the source of all things. This is understanding *wu* 無 as "to not have," parallel to *ci* 此 (this is) in the immediately following phrase.

14. Shima Kunio 島邦男, *Rōshi kōsei* 老子校正 (Tokyo: Kyūko shoin, 1973). The translation is from D. C. Lau, *Tao Te Ching* (Hong Kong: Chinese University Press, 1982).

15. Wangzi 王子 (Master Wang) is also known as Wang Ziqiao 王子喬, an immortal that the poetic persona encounters during his journey. The location of the encounter is specified in the preceding line: 順凱風以從游兮, 至南巢而壹息 "Drifting in the wake of the gentle south wind, I traveled to Nanchao in a single journey."

16. Hong Xingzu, *Chuci buzhu*, 139–40; and Hawkes, *The Songs of the South*, 168–69.

17. Note that "weaving this way and that" translates *shilu* 識路, which is read *zhiluo* 織絡 in a proposal by Wen Yiduo 聞一多 and accepted by Hawkes.

18. Old Chinese reconstructions are from Axel Schuessler, *Minimal Old Chinese and Later Han Chinese: A Companion to Grammata Serica Recensa* (Honolulu: University of Hawai'i Press, 2009), which is in turn based on William H. Baxter, *Handbook of Old Chinese Phonology* (Berlin: Mouton de Gruyter, 1992). For the purposes of this study, this is a simpler and for that reason more preferable reconstruction than Baxter's later collaboration with Laurent Sagart in *Old Chinese: A New Reconstruction* (Oxford: Oxford University Press, 2014).

19. Li Xueqin 李學勤, ed., *Maoshi zhengyi* 毛詩正義 (traditional character ed.; Beijing: Beijing daxue, 2000), 1025.

20. Hong Xingzu, *Chuci buzhu*, 265–67; and Hawkes, *The Songs of the South*, 266–67.

21. This is following Hong Xingzu in taking the pronunciation of 眐 to be *zheng* 征, since the former is not attested.

22. Following Sun Jingtao 孫景濤, my analysis of *yingning* as "fission reduplication" would identify *ying* as the "base" and *ning* the "reduplicant"; see Sun, *Gu Hanyu chongdie gouci fa yanjiu* 古漢語重疊構詞法研究 (Shanghai: Shanghai jiaoyu, 2008), 3–4.

23. Hong Xingzu, *Chuci buzhu*, 135–36.

24. Li Xueqin, ed., *Maoshi zhengyi*, 92; *Shuowen jiezi* (1873 woodblock ed.; Beijing: Zhonghua, 1963), 1b.18. Both of these are discussed, together with other examples, in my study: "Guodian zhujian 'Liude,' 'Wuxing' guanyu ren yi zhi ji de yizu cihui" 郭店竹簡《六德》、《五行》關於仁義之際的一組詞彙, *Zhongguo wenhua yanjiu suo xuebao* 中國文化研究所學報 [*Journal of Chinese Studies*] 59 (2014): 53–86; also my monograph, *The Lost Texts of Confucius's Grandson: Guodian, Zisi, and Beyond* (Hong Kong: The Chinese University Press, 2023), chap. 7.

25. For this usage, cf. the text in the *Zhuangzi* called "Xu Wugui" 徐无鬼, with the following statement: 君若勿已矣, 脩胸中之誠, 以應天地之情而勿攖 "If you must do something, cultivate the sincerity which is in your breast and use it to respond without opposition to the true form of heaven and earth"; see Wang Shumin, *Zhuangzi jiaoquan*, 926; and the translation in Watson, *The Complete Works of Chuang Tzu*, 264. In the text from the *Annals of Lü Buwei* (Lüshi chunqiu 呂氏春秋) called "Making Life the Foundation" (Ben sheng 本生), there is also the following: 能養天之所生而勿攖之, 謂天子 "The person who is capable of nurturing the life that heaven has created without doing violence to it is called the Son of Heaven"; see Chen Qiyou 陳奇猷, *Lüshi chunqiu xin jiaoshi* 呂氏春秋新校釋 (Shanghai: Shanghai guji, 2002), 21; and the translation in John Knoblock and Jeffrey Riegel, *The Annals of Lü Buwei: A Complete Translation and Study* (Stanford:

Stanford University Press, 2000), 64. Finally, in the text from the *Huainanzi* 淮南子 called "Quintessential Spirit" (Jingshen 精神), we find the statement: 抱其太清之本而無所容與, 而物無能營 "Embracing the foundation of grand purity without losing themselves, and things cannot disturb them"; see He Ning 何寧, *Huainanzi jishi* 淮南子集釋 (Beijing: Zhonghua, 1998), 523; and the translation from John S. Major, Sarah A. Queen, Andrew Seth Meyer, and Harold D. Roth, *Huainanzi: A Guide to the Theory and Practice of Government in Early Han China* (New York: Columbia University Press, 2010), 249. The usage of *ying* 營 in this last example is indistinguishable from *ying* 攖 in the other two texts. This is further evidence of the interchange between the two.

26. This and other familiar examples are cited in Hong Cheng 洪誠, *Xungu xue* 訓詁學 (Nanjing: Jiangsu guji, 2000), 91–92.

27. Qiu Xigui 裘錫圭, *Wenzi xue gaiyao* 文字學概要, 3rd ed. (Beijing: Shangwu, 2013), 246–47.

28. Wang Shumin, *Zhuangzi jiaoquan*, 652–57; and Watson, *The Complete Works of Chuang Tzu*, 194–95.

29. Wang Shumin, *Zhuangzi jiaoquan*, 714–18; Watson, *The Complete Works of Chuang Tzu*, 207–8.

30. In his comparison of the two passages, Wang Shumin cites Yu Yue's 俞樾 (1821–1907) observation that in its understanding of 委蛇 as *weishe* ("serpentine snake"), "Mastering Life" leaves behind a fragmentary phrase that is difficult to account for: 則平陸而已矣. This corresponds to the phrase from "Perfect Happiness": "to play among the banks and islands" (遊之壇陸), but in the context of "Mastering Life" it makes no sense at all, and Watson's translation as "then it can feel at ease" is as he himself admits rather tentative; see Watson, *The Complete Works of Chuang Tzu*, 208n12. Yu Yue goes on to suggest that "Mastering Life" should be emended on the basis of "Perfect Happiness." Although I agree with Yu Yue, there does not seem to be any reason to think that such "corruption" did not take place early on. Note that the authorities cited by Lu Deming 陸德明 (556–627) already understand the expression as *weishe* ("serpentine snake").

31. For another attestation of *weishe* as "serpentine snake," again seen in the *Zhuangzi*, we may turn to a different passage earlier in "Mastering Life": 委蛇, 其大如轂, 其長如轅, 紫衣而朱冠; 其為物也惡, 聞雷車之聲, 則捧其首而立, 見之者殆乎霸 "The *weishe* is as big as a wheel hub, as tall as a carriage shaft, has a purple robe and a vermilion hat and, as creatures go, is very ugly. When it hears the sound of thunder or a carriage, it grabs its head and stands up. Anyone who sees it will become a hegemon"; see Wang Shumin, *Zhuangzi jiaoquan*, 693–700; and the translation from Watson, *The Complete Works of Chuang Tzu*, 203–4. This passage is interesting for several reasons. For one, in its effort to give an explanation of *weishe*, it makes an interpretive move similar to "The Great and Venerable Teacher." This departs from the understanding of *weiyi* as a reduplicative word but embraces a body of lore about a serpentine snake. See, for instance, a passage from

the *Guideways through Mountains and Seas* (Shanhai jing 山海經) that describes a spirit named Yanwei 延維 in the following terms: 有人曰苗民; 有神焉, 人首蛇身, 長如轅, 左右有首, 衣紫衣, 冠旃冠, 名曰延維; 人主得而饗食之, 伯天下 "There are the Miao people. There is a spirit among them that has human heads and the body of a snake. It is as tall as a carriage shaft, has heads on the left and right, wears a purple robe and a red hat. It is named Yanwei. If a ruler gets to feast on it, he will be a hegemon for all under heaven"; see Yuan Ke 袁珂, *Shanhai jing jiaozhu* 山海經校注, 2nd ed. (Chengdu: Ba Shu, 1992), 518–19. For this and other related lore about the serpentine snake, identified in the literary record also as Weiwei 委維, Feiyi 肥遺, Feiyi 肥蠵, Gui 蟡, and Yu'er 俞兒, see the set of short articles by Huang Yongnian 黃永年 in *Huang Yongnian wenshi lunwen ji* 黃永年文史論文集 (Beijing: Zhonghua, 2015), especially "Shenhua zhong de yizhong guaishe—'Weishe'" 神話中的一種怪蛇——「委蛇」, in 4: 18–21. Comparing the two texts, it seems to me that the author of "Mastering Life" took the *Guideways through Mountains and Seas* or a tradition closely related to it and replaced the name Yanwei with *weishe*. The reason I suggest this, rather than the other way around, is that I observe a similar relation between "Perfect Happiness" and the first passage from "Mastering Life": the latter took the name *qiuchou* 鰌鰷 ("mudfish and minnows") and replaced it with *weishe* ("serpentine snake"). In both cases, "Mastering Life" is allowing for its literal understanding of *weishe* to replace an expression that is more unusual or otherwise unattested, be it *qiuchou* or *Yanwei*. This relation is consistent with the suggestion by Yu Yue mentioned in the previous footnote, that "Mastering Life" is based on "Perfect Happiness."

32. Jiao Xun 焦循, *Mengzi zhengyi* 孟子正義 (Beijing: Zhonghua, 1987), 775–78; and the translation in D. C. Lau, *Mencius*, 2nd ed. (Hong Kong: Chinese University of Hong Kong Press, 2003).

33. "Far-off Journey" also has the line: 餐六氣而飲沆瀣兮, 漱正陽而含朝霞 "I supped the Six Essences; drank the Night Dew; rinsed my mouth in the Sun Mist; savored the Morning Brightness." Hawkes's translation of "night dew" is evidently based on Zhang Xian's 張銑 (ca. 718) commentary on the "Rhapsody on the Zither (Qinfu 琴賦), as seen in the *Selections of Refined Literature* (Wenxuan 文選), where *hangxie* 沆瀣 is glossed as *qinglu* 清露 "clear dew"; see *Liuchen zhu Wenxuan* 六臣注文選 (woodblock edition from ca. 1131–1162; Beijing: Zhonghua, 1987), 18.23. This is different from, but not entirely irreconcilable with the standard view that *hangxie* is a certain "*qi* of the midnight double-hour in the North" (*beifang yeban qi* 北方夜半氣), such as given in Wang Yi's commentary (who is in turn citing a work called the *Lingyangzi mingjing* 陵陽子明經) and echoed by Ying Shao 應劭 (ca. 140–before 204) and Lu Deming in different contexts; see Wang Xianqian 王先謙, *Hanshu buzhu* 漢書補注 (Shanghai: Shanghai guji, 2008), 4189, and Huang Zhuo 黃焯, *Jingdian shiwen huijiao* 經典釋文彙校 (Beijing: Zhonghua, 2006), 26.3b. For a nod toward Zhang Xian's view, see Inui Kazuo 乾一夫, "Mōshi to yaki setsu—Nikutai no yōjō to seishinteki kyūyō no aida" 孟子と夜気説——肉体の養生と精神

的休養のあいだ, in *Seiken no genzō: Chūgoku kodai shisō kenkyū josetsu* 聖賢の原像: 中国古代思想研究序説 (Tokyo: Meiji Shoin, 1988), 279–308. Inui comments insightfully that the imbibing of dew, a kind of crystallization of *yeqi* or the air of the night, is widely attested in the literary record; it can be found, for instance, in the description of the "divine man" (*shenren* 神人) in the *Zhuangzi* text "Free and Easy Wandering" (Xiaoyao you 逍遙遊). As for "Far-off Journey" itself, note that the reference to *hangxie* is followed immediately by the line: 保神明之清澄兮, 精氣入而麤穢除 "Conserving the pure elements of the divine; absorbing the subtle essence and rejecting the grosser parts." This corresponds to the discussion in the Mawangdui 馬王堆 text "Ten Questions" (Shiwen 十問), which I discuss immediately below.

34. Qiu Xigui 裘錫圭, ed., *Changsha Mawangdui Hanmu jianbo jicheng* 長沙馬王堆漢墓簡帛集成 (Beijing: Zhonghua, 2014), 2: 203–11, and the transcription in 6: 139–51. The translation is based on Donald Harper, *Early Chinese Medical Literature: The Mawangdui Medical Manuscripts* (London: Kegan Paul International, 1997), 393–99. Note also another text from Mawangdui, "Sixteen Canons" (Shiliujing 十六經). In a section entitled "Observation" (Guan 觀), "air of the night" (*yeqi*) is defined (lines 85a–86b) as *bi di yun zhe* 閉地繩 (孕) 者 ("what impregnates under buried grounds"), a force of generation associated with *yang* (as opposed to *yin*) and *de* 德 (as opposed to *xing* 刑); see Qiu Xigui, ed., *Changsha Mawangdui Hanmu jianbo jicheng*, 1: 129–30, and the transcription in 4: 152–55. Cf. the translation in Robin D. S. Yates, *Five Lost Classics: Tao, Huanglao, and Yin-yang in Han China* (New York: Ballantine Books, 1997), 106–11. Interestingly, this comment comes from the mouth of Li Hei 力黑, an emissary of the Yellow Emperor who "moves about in secret, under cover" (*qianxing funi* 侵 (潛) 行伏匿) in order to observe the world. I explore *qianxing* 潛行 and other related expressions in chapter 4.

35. For another reference to the physiological basis for the conception of *qi* discussed here, see a text from the *Luxuriant Gems of the Spring and Autumn* (Chunqiu fanlu 春秋繁露) called "Conform to Heaven's Way" (Xun tian zhi dao 循天之道), which has the following statement: 鶴之所以壽者, 無宛氣於中, 是故食不凝 "The reason that a crane lives long is that it has no congestion of *qi* inside its body. Thus the food it ingests does not coagulate." This corresponds to a quotation of the *Luxuriant Gems of the Spring and Autumn* cited in the medieval encyclopedia *Notes for Young Beginners* (Chuxueji 初學記), in the section on cranes: 鶴知夜半, 鶴所以壽者, 無死氣於中也 "The crane knows about midnight. The reason that a crane lives long is that it has no dead *qi* inside its body." Here, "midnight" (*yeban* 夜半) refers to the midnight double-hour and the kind of breathing exercise that takes place at that time; see Su Yu 蘇輿, *Chunqiu fanlu jizheng* 春秋繁露集證 (Beijing: Zhonghua, 1992), 449; and *Chuxueji* 初學記 (Beijing: Zhonghua, 1962), *juan* 30, 726. Cf. Sarah A. Queen and John S. Major, *Luxuriant Gems of the Spring and Autumn* (New York: Columbia University Press, 2016), 575.

Chapter 2

1. This reading is first proposed by Cao Feng in his article "'Fan wu liu xing' 'xin bu sheng xin' zhang shuzheng"《凡物流形》「心不勝心」章疏證, in *Jinnian chutu Huang Lao sixiang wenxian yanjiu*, 328–40. Besides the connection with "The Great and Venerable Teacher," Cao's study shares with my own the focus on the same passage from "All Things Flow into Form," though it seems to me that Cao leaves too many details unexplained. One case in point is the pronunciations of *shao* 少 (*hjau) and *zhao* 朝 (*trau). While Cao is correct to observe that both words belong to the same Old Chinese rhyme group *xiao* 宵, it remains that the initials of the two words need to be accounted for. Here, I would suggest that the phonetics of the two words appear to be interchangeable with *zhou* 周 (*tiu). For example, the poem "Bank of the Ru Stream" (Rufen 汝墳) in the *Book of Odes* has the line: "While I have not seen the lord, I am desirous as if morning-hungry" (未見君子, 惄如調飢); see Li Xueqin, ed., *Maoshi zhengyi*, 68; and the translation from Bernhard Karlgren, *The Book of Odes: Chinese Text, Transcription and Translation* (Stockholm: Museum of Far Eastern Antiquities, 1950), 7. In the quotation of this line in the ancient dictionary *Explaining Graphs and Analyzing Characters*, *tiao* 調 is given as *zhao* 朝; see *Shuowen jiezi* 10b.15. This, in fact, is one of the reasons behind Karlgren's translation, though he objects to the view that one might be the phonetic loan of the other; see his *Glosses on the Book of Odes* (Stockholm: Museum of Far Eastern Antiquities, 1964), #35. Karlgren's objection notwithstanding, we may consider another example of the interchange in the *History of the Former Han* (Hanshu 漢書). According to the biography of Dongfang Shou 東方朔 (fl. 130 BCE), this man waited upon the emperor with several others, "playing the jester, and nothing more" (*huizhao eryi* 詼啁而已). For this, Yan Shigu 顏師古 (581–645) comments that *zhao* 啁 is identical with *chao* 嘲; see Wang Xianqian 王先謙, *Hanshu buzhu* 漢書補注 (Shanghai: Shanghai guji, 2008), 4532–33; and the translation in Burton Watson, *Courtier and Commoner in Ancient China: Selections from the History of the Former Han by Pan Ku* (New York: Columbia University Press, 1974), 96. In terms of *shao* 少, a poem from the *Book of Odes* called "Good Ploughs" (*Liangsi* 良耜) has the line: "Their hoes pierce the ground, to clear away *tu* plants and smartweed" (其鎛斯趙, 以薅荼蓼); see Li Xueqin, ed., *Maoshi zhengyi*, 1601; and the translation in Karlgren, *The Book of Odes*, 251. This is cited in Zheng Xuan's 鄭玄 (127–200) commentary to "Records of the Scrutiny of Crafts" (*Kaogongji* 考工記), with *zhao* 挑 in the place of *diao* 趙; see Sun Yirang 孫詒讓, *Zhouli zhengyi* 周禮正義 (Beijing: Zhonghua, 1987), 3111. All of this suggests a close phonological relation among *shao* 少 (*hjau), 周 (*tiu), and *zhao* 朝 (*trau), an example of the kind of logical relation where if *a* is similar to *b*, and *b* is similar to *c*, then it is possible that *a* is also similar to *c*. In other words, it would have been possible for the word *zhao* 朝 to be written with the character *shao* 少. For another example of

this in paleographic texts, consider the "Rongchengshi" 容成氏, another Warring States manuscript in the Shanghai Museum collection, where one finds the following account about King Wu's conquest of the Shang (slips 51–52): 武王乃出革車五百輬 (乘), 縶 (帶) 摩 (甲) 三千, 吕 (以) 少 (朝) 會者 (諸) 矦 (侯) 之帀 (師) 於臸 (牧) 之埜 (野) "King Wu then sent out five hundred war chariots and three thousand armored warriors, and in the morning joined the troops of the feudal lords at the open ground outside of Mu"; see Ma Chengyuan, ed., *Shanghai Bowuguan cang Zhanguo Chu zhushu*, vol. 2; and the translation modified from Sarah Allan, *Buried Ideas: Legends of Abdication and Ideal Government in Early Chinese Bamboo-Slip Manuscripts* (Albany: State University of New York Press), 258. Here, as is consistent with my treatment of "All Things Flow into Form," I read the character *shao* as *zhao*. This has the support of most accounts of this celebrated event, which describes King Wu's convening and rallying of his allies, on the day of the battle, in broad daylight. While some scholars have proposed reading *shao* as *xiao* 宵 ("night"), it seems to me that the kind of clandestine activity implied by this term is not suitable for the context of the very "Rongchengshi" passage concerned. See, for example, Chen Wei 陳偉, "Shanghai bowuguan cang Zhanguo Chu zhushu (er) lingshi" 《上海博物館藏戰國楚竹書》(二) 零釋, in *Xinchu Chujian yandu* 新出楚簡研讀 (Wuhan: Wuhan daxue, 2010), 144–45. The translation by Allan cited above reads *shao* as it is, understanding it to refer to the lesser amount of the troops of the feudal lords, but this is grammatically difficult to construe, and for that reason I have modified it according to my own understanding.

2. We may compare this kind of transparency with a text from the *Annals of Lü Buwei* (Lüshi chunqiu) called "Supreme Virtue" (Shangde 上德), which contains the following description of ideal rulers: 故古之王者, 德迴乎天地, 澹乎四海, 東西南北, 極日月之所燭, 天覆地載, 愛惡不臧, 虛素以公 "Hence, when the kings of antiquity ruled, their Power penetrated Heaven and Earth, reaching to the four seas, east, west, south, and north, to the farthest places illuminated by the sun and moon. They covered all like Heaven, supported all like Earth, harbored neither love nor hate, and, being empty and plain, were fair-minded"; see Chen Qiyou, *Lüshi chunqiu xin jiaoshi*, 1264–65; and the translation from Knoblock and Riegel, *The Annals of Lü Buwei: A Complete Translation and Study*, 484–85. Following a proposal by Wang Niansun 王念孫 (1744–1832), I read *dong* 迴 ("to penetrate") as opposed to *hui* 迴 ("to circulate"), and I have modified the translation accordingly; see Chen Qiyou, *Lüshi chunqiu xin jiaoshi*, 935–36. As given here, *gong* 公 is "fair-minded" but also the casting aside of any private and selfish interests, so one resembles, in effect, Heaven, Earth, and other forces of nature. Of course, *su* is a synonym of *bai*. The two words are juxtaposed in one of the poems mentioned in chapter 1, "Alas That My Lot Was Not Cast" (Ai shiming): 形體白而質素兮, 中皎潔而淑清 "I am clean in my body and pure in substance; my soul within is dazzling in its spotless purity"; see Hong Xingzu, *Chuci buzhu*, 265–67; and Hawkes, *The Songs*

of the South, 266–67. See also the passages from the *Han Feizi* 韓非子 cited later in the chapter.

3. Photographs of the manuscripts, together with transcriptions, can be found in *Guodian Chumu zhujian* 郭店楚墓竹簡 (Beijing: Wenwu, 1998). Among later studies, two notable works are *Guodian Chumu zhushu* 郭店楚墓竹書 (*Chudi chutu Zhanguo jiance heji* 楚地出土戰國簡冊合集, vol. 1; Beijing: Wenwu, 2011); and the English translation by Scott Cook, *The Bamboo Texts of Guodian: A Study and Complete Translation* (Ithaca: East Asia Program, Cornell University, 2012). Both are critical editions that reflect more recent research on the texts.

4. For a more detailed discussion of "Grand One Gives Birth to Water," see *The Lost Texts of Confucius's Grandson*, chap. 4.

5. Zhu Xi, *Zhongyong zhangju* 中庸章句, in *Sishu zhangju jizhu* 四書章句集注 (Beijing: Zhonghua, 1983), 14–40. In Zhu Xi's reckoning, among a total of thirty-three sections in the "Zhongyong," *cheng* appears only in sections 16, 20–26, and 32. See also the summary of various proposals in Jeffrey K. Riegel, "The Four 'Tzu Ssu' Chapters of the *Li Chi*: An Analysis and Translation of the *Fang Chi*, *Chung Yung*, *Piao Chi*, and *Tzu I*," PhD diss., Stanford University, 1978, 74–109.

6. Jiao Xun, *Mengzi zhengyi*, 508–12, 882–84.

7. To be more specific, in acknowledging the importance of the Way of Heaven with which *cheng* is closely aligned, Mencius suggests that it is human action that truly matters. I discuss these passages in *The Lost Texts of Confucius's Grandson*, chap. 8.

8. See *The Lost Texts of Confucius's Grandson*, chap. 1.

9. Wang Shumin, *Zhuangzi jiaoquan*, 885–94. The translation is modified from Watson, *The Complete Works of Chuang Tzu*, 254–56.

10. Here the word *bei* 備 ("to prepare") corresponds to not only the immediately following *cang* 藏 ("to store") but, more importantly, the discussion in the same passage of a *lingtai* 靈臺 ("spirit tower"), defined as the following by "Gengsang Chu": 有持而不知其所持而不可持者也 "It holds but does not know what it holds cannot be held." In fact, the theme of the holding of things appears again later in the discussion of the merchant (*guren* 賈人) who *zhi hu qi fei* 志乎期費 ("sets his mind on spending lavishly"), which "Gengsang Chu" rejects.

11. This last phrase restored, following Wang Shumin.

12. Cf. the discussion in another text from the *Zhuangzi*, "In the World of Men" (Renjianshi 人間世), concerning *xushi sheng bai* 虛室生白 ("the empty chamber with a glowing light"); see Wang Shumin, *Zhuangzi jiaoquan*, 117–36; and the translation in Watson, *The Complete Works of Chuang Tzu*, 54–58. This oxymoron (an unoccupied residence should not emit any light) appears as a metaphor for the mind: the emptying of one's mind (what is called *xinzhai* 心齋, "the fasting of the mind," earlier in the same passage) allows spirits to enter into oneself and endows one with their powers. I discuss other related oxymorons later in the book.

13. Li Xueqin, ed., *Liji zhengyi* 禮記正義 (traditional character ed.; Beijing: Beijing daxue, 2000), 1859–66. The translation is modified from Wing-tsit Chan, *A Source Book in Chinese Philosophy* (Princeton: Princeton University Press, 1963), 89–90.

14. Cf. the discussion in "Gengsang Chu" about emitting a heavenly light, such that "people will be seen for what they are and things will be seen for what they are."

15. As for the comparison of the body to a house in the first part of the statement, this is also reminiscent of "Gengsang Chu," particularly the phrase, *yu taiding zhe* 宇泰定者 ("He whose inner being rests in the great serenity"). While *yu* 宇 is literally the eaves of a house, or "boundary" more generally, in "Gengsang Chu" it is used metaphorically to refer to the place where the mind is lodged. A similar metaphor from the same text is *lingtai* ("spirit tower"), as mentioned earlier. See also the reference to a *xushi* 虛室 ("empty chamber") in "In the World of Men," also noted earlier. Finally, in "Inner Workings" (Neiye 內業) and other related texts in the *Guanzi*, we find the key word *she* 舍 ("lodging") as a storage place for one's *jing* 精 ("vital essence"), *qi* 氣, and *shen* 神 ("spirit").

16. It is not difficult to see that *zi qi* ("to cheat oneself") from "Great Learning" is comparable to the following expressions from Mencius: *zi zei* 自賊 ("to cripple oneself") in 2A6, and *zi bao* 自暴 ("to have no respect for oneself") and *zi qi* 自棄 ("to have no confidence in oneself"), both 4A10; see Jiao Xun, *Mengzi zhengyi*, 232–36, 507–8. Cf. also Xunzi's essay "Dispelling Blindness" (Jie bi 解蔽), which I will discuss in chapter 4: 心者, 形之君也, 而神明之主也, 出令而無所受令, 自禁也, 自使也, 自奪也, 自取也, 自行也, 自止也 "The mind is the lord of the body and master of the spiritual intelligence. It issues commands but does not receive commands. On its own authority it forbids or orders, renounces or selects, initiates or stops." See Wang Xianqian 王先謙, Kubo Ai 久保愛, Ikai Hikohiro 猪飼彥博, Hattori Unokichi 服部宇之吉, *Junshi* 荀子 (Kanbun taikei, vol. 15; Tokyo: Fuzanbō, 1913), 15.14. The translation is modified from John Knoblock, *Xunzi: A Translation and Study of the Complete Works* (Stanford: Stanford University Press, 1988–94), 3: 105. These are the negative consequences from the mind's being blinded by too many distractions, or to use the metaphor employed by Xunzi himself, when the authority of the mind is thwarted by the senses.

17. Cf. Kong Yingda's 孔穎達 (574–678) commentary, where he paraphrases *zi qie* as *qieran anjing zhi mao* 慊然安靜之貌 ("the appearance of being satisfied and quiet"). This even more explicitly connects *zi qie* and *zi ruo*.

18. Samuel P. Huntington, *American Politics: The Promise of Disharmony* (Cambridge, MA: Belknap Press, 1981), 75.

19. Chen Qiyou 陳奇猷, *Han Feizi xin jiaozhu* 韓非子新校注 (Shanghai: Shanghai guji, 2000), 145–52. The translation is modified from W. K. Liao, "(Liao Wenkui 廖文魁)" *The Complete Works of Han Fei Tzǔ: A Classic of Chinese Political Science* (London: Arthur Probsthain, 1959), 1: 53. Chen Qiyou draws attention to

an earlier phrase from the same text: 權不欲見, 素無為也, which can be emended to the following: 情不欲見; 素, 無為也 "One does not wish to have reality revealed; *su* ["plainness"] is nonaction." Chen believes this was originally part of the commentary for the passage under discussion.

20. The character 令 deleted, following Chen Qiyou and the scholars cited by him.

21. The characters *jiu* 舊 and *zhi* 智 reversed, following Wang Niansun. The former (*gwəʔ/h) rhymes with *bei* 備 (*brekh) in the following phrase, likely the reason that it is used rather than its more common synonym *gu* 故.

22. Chen Qiyou, *Han Feizi xin jiaozhu*, 66–74; and the translation from W. K. Liao, *The Complete Works of Han Fei Tzǔ*, 1: 30–31.

23. Chen Qiyou, *Han Feizi xin jiaozhu*, 130–37; and the translation from W. K. Liao, *The Complete Works of Han Fei Tzǔ*, 1: 51.

24. For another example of this usage of *su*, note that "Doctrine of the Mean" has the following statement: 君子素其位而行, 不願乎其外 "The superior man does what is proper to his position and does not want to go beyond this"; see Li Xueqin, ed., *Liji zhengyi*, 1661–712. The translation is from Wing-tsit Chan, *A Source Book in Chinese Philosophy*, 101.

25. Chen Qiyou, *Han Feizi xin jiaozhu*, 973–74; and the translation from W. K. Liao, *The Complete Works of Han Fei Tzǔ*, 2: 220. A parallel to this passage can be found in a text from the *Garden of Sayings* (Shuoyuan 說苑) called "The Art of the Minister" (Chenshu 臣術). Like its counterpart from Han Feizi, this passage enumerates the different types of ministers and describes one of them as the following: 二曰虛心白意, 進善通道, 勉主以禮義, 諭主以長策, 將順其美, 匡救其惡, 功成事立, 歸善於君, 不敢獨伐其勞, 如此者良臣也 "The second is emptying the mind and revealing one's intention, advancing goodness and getting through to the Way, encouraging one's ruler with propriety, illuminating him with plans with long-term prospects, complying with his fine qualities, correcting the bad ones, and when there are successes and accomplishments, they are ascribed to the lord and one dares not boast of one's labor—such would be a good minister"; see Zuo Songchao 左松超, *Shuoyuan jizheng* 說苑集證 (Taipei: Guoli bianyi guan, 2000), 91–99.

26. Li Xueqin, ed., *Qinghua daxue cang Zhanguo zhujian* 清華大學藏戰國竹簡 (Shanghai: Zhong Xi, 2016), vol. 6.

Chapter 3

1. Ma Chengyuan, ed., *Shanghai Bowuguan cang Zhanguo Chu zhushu*, vol. 5. For studies of this text, see Gu Shikao 顧史考 (Scott Cook), "Shangbo Chujian 'Junzi wei li' zaitan" 上博楚簡《君子為禮》再探, paper presented at the Zhongguo Wenzixue Guoji Xueshu Yantaohui 中國文字學國際學術研討會, May 18–19, 2018; Hou Naifeng 侯乃峰, *Shangbo Chujian Ruxue wenxian jiaoli* 上博楚簡儒學文獻校理

(Shanghai: Shanghai guji, 2018), 244–54; and the annotations by Imata Hiroshi 今田裕志 in Yanaka Shin'ichi 谷中信一, ed., *Chūgoku shutsudo shiryō no takakuteki kenkyū* 中国出土資料の多角的研究 (Tokyo: Kyūko shoin, 2018), 53–77. For the *Analects* 12.1, a work that brings together much of the relevant modern scholarship on this text is Xiang Shiling 向世陵, ed., "*Ke ji fu li wei ren*" *yanjiu yu zhengming* 「克己復禮為仁」研究與爭鳴 (Beijing: Xinxing, 2018).

2. For my discussion in this chapter, I have been much inspired by Zhou Fengwu's 周鳳五 insightful analysis of Mencius 2A2, particularly the statement: 是集義所生者，非義襲而取之也 "[*Qi*] is born of accumulated rightness and cannot be appropriated by anyone through a sporadic show of rightness"; see "Shangbo 'Xingqing lun' 'Jinshi zhi yousheng ye, fu kou bu ming' jie" 上博《性情論》「金石之有聲也，弗叩不鳴」解, in *Pengzhai xueshu wenji: Zhanguo zhushu juan* 朋齋學術文集：戰國竹書卷 (Taipei: Taiwan daxue, 2016), 211–17.

3. Cheng Shude 程樹德, *Lunyu jishi* 論語集釋 (Beijing: Zhonghua, 1990), 817–24; and the translation from D. C. Lau, *The Analects* (Hong Kong: Chinese University Press, 1992).

4. Yang Bojun 楊伯峻, *Chunqiu Zuozhuan zhu* 春秋左傳注 (Beijing: Zhonghua, 1981), 1338–41. The translation is modified from Stephen Durrant, Wai-yee Li, and David Schaberg, *Zuo Traditions = Zuozhuan: Commentary on the "Spring and Autumn Annals"* (Seattle: University of Washington Press, 2016), 1481–85.

5. Chen Qiyou, *Han Feizi xin jiaozhu*, 460. The translation is modified from W. K. Liao, *The Complete Works of Han Fei Tzǔ*, 1: 226. Besides the passages discussed hereafter, another reference to Zixia can be found in the *Grand Scribe's Records* (Shiji 史記), in "The Treatise on the Calendars" (Lishu 曆書); see Takigawa Kametarō and Mizusawa Toshitada, *Shiji huizhu kaozheng fu jiaobu*, 23.4–5. For another quotation, see the text in the *Wenzi* 文子 called "Debased Virtues" (Xiade 下德). This and the relevant discussion in another text, "Matching Words" (Fuyan 符言) can be found in Wang Liqi 王利器, *Wenzi shuyi* 文子疏義 (Beijing: Zhonghua, 2000), 388–91, 207–8. Other related passages are in the text from the *Huainanzi* called "The Exalted Lineage" (Taizu 泰族) and "Sayings Explained" (Quanyan 詮言); see He Ning, *Huainanzi jishi*, 1413–18, 995–98. Briefly, these discussions all use language similar to the passages considered here, but they also point to a broader issue: the ruler should cultivate himself before winning the support of others. This anticipates a point about "The Gentlemen Enact the Rites" that I will consider presently.

6. Shima Kunio, *Rōshi kōsei*.

7. Shima Kunio, *Rōshi kōsei*. The translation is from Eduard Erkes, *Ho-Shang-Kung's Commentary on Lao-Tse* (Ascona: Artibus Asiae, 1950).

8. Li Xueqin, ed., *Liji zhengyi*, 1859–66. The translation is modified from Wing-tsit Chan, *A Source Book in Chinese Philosophy*, 89–90.

9. The character *bu* 不 added, following Wang Niansun.

10. The character *yi* 宜 deleted, following Wang Niansun.

11. He Ning, *Huainanzi jishi*, 547–54. The translation is modified from Major et al., *Huainanzi*, 259.

12. See also the related discussion in the text from the *Huainanzi* called "Originating in the Way" (Yuandao 原道), in He Ning, *Huainanzi jishi*, 66–90.

13. Related passages can be found in the text from the *Annals of Lü Buwei* called "Being Attentive to the Purposes of Action" (Shen wei 審為), in Chen Qiyou, *Lüshi chunqiu xin jiaoshi*, 1464; in the text in the *Huainanzi* called "Responses of the Way" (Daoying 道應), in He Ning, *Huainanzi jishi*, 849–50; and in the text in the *Wenzi* called "Debased Virtues" (Xiade), in Wang Liqi, *Wenzi shuyi*, 384–85.

14. The reading of *chong* (*pingsheng* 平聲 or "level tone" in Middle Chinese) follows Yu Yue, who has the support of Gao You 高誘 (ca. 168–212) under the passage from the *Annals of Lü Buwei*, cited in the previous footnote.

15. Wang Shumin, *Zhuangzi jiaoquan*, 1148–51. The translation is slightly modified from Watson, *The Complete Works of Chuang Tzu*, 317–18.

16. A. C. Graham, "The Background of the Mencian Theory of Human Nature," in *Studies in Chinese Philosophy and Philosophical Literature* (Singapore: Institute of East Asian Philosophies, 1986), 7–66.

17. The latest example of this is the Warring States manuscript "The Mind Is What Is Internal to Oneself" (Xin shi wei zhong 心是謂中) from the Tsinghua University collection; see Li Xueqin, ed., *Qinghua daxue cang Zhanguo zhujian* (Shanghai: Zhong Xi, 2018), vol. 8.

18. Chen Qiyou, *Lüshi chunqiu xin jiaoshi*, 21. The translation is modified from Knoblock and Riegel, *The Annals of Lü Buwei*, 64.

19. Chen Qiyou, *Lüshi chunqiu xin jiaoshi*, 22. The translation is from Knoblock and Riegel, *The Annals of Lü Buwei*, 66–67.

20. On this last point, cf. another text from the *Annals of Lü Buwei*, "Stressing the Self" (*Zhong ji* 重己), also identified a Yangist text by Graham: 凡生之長也, 順之也; 使生不順者, 欲也; 故聖人必先適欲 "As a general principle, the prolongation of life results from one's following its natural course and what causes one not to follow the natural course of life is desire. Thus, the sage is certain to give priority to making his desires suitable"; see Chen Qiyou, *Lüshi chunqiu xin jiaoshi*, 35; and the translation from Knoblock and Riegel, *The Annals of Lü Buwei: A Complete Translation and Study*, 68–9. The passage mentioned above from the text in the *Huainanzi* called "Originating in the Way" (*Yuandao*) also contains the statement: 是故有以自得之也, 喬木之下, 空穴之中, 足以適情 "Therefore, if one has possession of himself, beneath the lofty trees and in empty caves, he will have what it takes to respond appropriately to his situation"; see He Ning, *Huainanzi jishi*, 66–90. The translation is modified from Major et al., *Huainanzi*, 68–69.

21. Jiao Xun, *Mengzi zhengyi*, 775–78.

22. Cf. the narrative from the *Zuo Tradition* cited at the beginning of this chapter, which uses the expression "to give free rein to the desires of one's heart" (*si qi xin*) to describe the kind of behavior that one should overcome.

23. The latter, of course, is the same word translated as "propriety" in "The Gentlemen Enact the Rites."

24. Jiao Xun, *Mengzi zhengyi*, 789–92, 792–95. The translations are from Lau, *Mencius*.

25. The classic study of these formulations is Kanaya Osamu 金谷治, "Shin no jū no shin—Chūgoku kodai shinrisetsu no tenkai" 心の中の心―中国古代心理説の展開, in *Chūgoku kodai no shizenkan to ningenkan* 中国古代の自然観と人間観 (Tokyo: Hirakawa, 1997), 353–67.

26. Li Xiangfeng 黎翔鳳, *Guanzi jiaozhu* 管子校注 (Beijing: Zhonghua, 2004), 937–42, 786–87.

27. Li Xueqin, ed., *Liji zhengyi*, 855–87. For "Five Conducts," the most relevant discussion can be found in the commentary portion of the Mawangdui text, line 96–97; see Qiu Xigui, ed., *Changsha Mawangdui Hanmu jianbo jicheng*, 1: 107; and the transcription in 4: 81–83.

28. See Huang, *The Lost Texts of Confucius's Grandson*, especially chap. 1.

29. Wang Shumin, *Zhuangzi jiaoquan*, 171–79. The translation has consulted Watson, *The Complete Works of Chuang Tzu*, 68–69, which follows a different version of the text: 受命於天，唯堯舜獨也正，在萬物之首 "Of those that receive life from Heaven, Yao and Shun alone are best—they stand at the head of the ten thousand things."

30. The example of this kind of repetition most familiar to readers will doubtless be the opening chapter of the *Laozi*. In fact, the contrast between the Way (*Dao* 道) and a more preferable "Constant Way" (*Changdao* 常道) corresponds to what one finds in "The Sign of Virtue Complete." My own take is to regard the *Laozi* passage as being modeled after "The Sign of Virtue Complete," for a reason similar to what I suggested earlier about the maxim, "Return to the observance of the rites through overcoming oneself" (*ke ji fu li*): the *Laozi* passage is so remarkable that it would have been odd for "The Sign of Virtue Complete" to not refer to it. That this *Zhuangzi* text does not do so hints at the possibility that it has an earlier date than the *Laozi* passage. This is consistent with the fact that the opening chapter does not figure in the Guodian texts (ca. fourth century BCE), which contain the earliest manuscripts related to the *Laozi*.

31. See, for instance, Lau, *Mencius*, 62n3. Cf. David S. Nivison's brief comparison of the two texts in "The Classical Philosophical Writings," in Edward L. Shaughnessy and Michael Loewe, eds., *The Cambridge History of Ancient China: From the Origins of Civilization to 221 B.C.* (Cambridge: Cambridge University Press, 1998), 784–86; also Nivison's earlier paper, "Philosophical Voluntarism in Fourth Century China," in *The Ways of Confucianism: Investigations in Chinese Philosophy* (Chicago: Open Court, 1996), 128–30.

32. Putting Mencius before Zhuangzi would also explain the reference to the mind in the passage from "The Sign of Virtue Complete" on the one hand, and the suggestion that Wang Tai "regards the loss of a foot as a lump of earth thrown away" (*shi sang qi zu you yitu ye* 視喪其足猶遺土也). The contrast between the mind and the foot is consistent with Mencius's distinction between the "greater" (*dati*) and "lesser" body (*xiaoti*).

33. Chen Qiyou, *Lüshi chunqiu xin jiaoshi*, 1235–36. The translation is from Knoblock and Riegel, *The Annals of Lü Buwei*, 470–72.

34. The classic study of this figure is Gustav Haloun, "Fragmente des Fu-tsï und des Tśiń-tsï: Frühkonfuzianische fragmente I," *Asia Major* 8 (1932): 437–509.

35. This is done, presumably, for conservation purposes.

36. He Ning, *Huainanzi jishi*, 890–91. The character *cheng* is emended from 誠, following Wang Niansun.

37. Jiang Lihong 蔣禮鴻, *Shangjun shu zhuizhi* 商君書錐指 (Beijing: Zhonghua, 1986), 110–13. The translation has consulted Yuri Pines, *The Book of Lord Shang: Apologetics of State Power in Early China* (New York: Columbia University Press, 2017), 219.

38. On the surface, this seems to conflict with Han Feizi's recommendation that the ruler should conceal his desires, as we saw in the passages cited in the previous chapter. But the two thinkers are alike in their focus on the desires of the ruler, which consequently leaves no room for the consideration of the desires of the subjects. On such basis, the question pursued is what the ruler should do about his desires.

39. Takigawa Kametarō and Mizusawa Toshitada, *Shiji huizhu kaozheng fu jiaobu*, 68.13–19. The translation is modified from William H. Nienhauser Jr., ed., *The Grand Scribe's Records* (Bloomington: Indiana University Press, 1994–), 7: 93. Formally, Zhao's comment resembles a text from the *Han Feizi* called "The Outer Congeries of Sayings, The Upper Right Series" (Waichu shuo you shang 外儲說右上), which contains the following quotation of Shenzi 申子 (ca. 400 BCE): 獨視者謂明, 獨聽者謂聰; 能獨斷者, 故可以為天下主 "Who sees things by himself is called clear-sighted; who hears things by himself is called acute; and who can make decision by himself is fit to rule all under Heaven"; see Chen Qiyou, *Han Feizi xin jiaozhu*, 783–84. The translation is modified from W. K. Liao, *The Complete Works of Han Fei Tzŭ*, 2: 104–5. In terms of actual content, the two could not be farther apart.

40. The same passage from "Charting the Policies" also contains the following statement: 仁者能仁於人, 而不能使人仁; 義者能愛於人, 而不能使人愛; 是以知仁義之不足以治天下也 "The benevolent can behave benevolently toward others but cannot make them benevolent; the righteous can love others but cannot make them love. From this I know that benevolence and righteousness are not sufficient to rule the world." And it ends with the following: 聖王者不貴義而貴法, 法必明, 令必行, 則已矣 "Sage kings did not esteem righteousness but esteemed the law: laws must be

clear; orders must be implemented—and that is all." The reference to "benevolence" (*ren*) and "righteousness" (*yi*) spells out what it is going against; see Jiang Lihong, *Shangjun shu zhuizhi*, 110–13. The translation is modified from Pines, *The Book of Lord Shang: Apologetics of State Power in Early China*, 220.

41. The interpretation of "The Gentlemen Enact the Rites" supplied here can also allow us to reexamine the *Zuo Tradition* narrative cited at the beginning of the chapter. Before the comment by Confucius, there is the adviser's criticism of the Chu ruler, but even before that there is an entire section where the adviser simply echoes the Chu ruler's words. The adviser's justification for this is that he was preparing the ruler for the criticism to follow, but perhaps this is only one possible explanation that happens to come out from the mouth of one of the main protagonists. In another version of the narrative, now found in the *Grand Scribe's Records*, there is only the part with the echoing, but not the criticism, and this results in a very different overall narrative than what appears in the *Zuo Tradition*. In light of the discussion here, I would propose reading the two parts of the *Zuo Tradition* as two units: the first is an instance where the ruler's power dominates the subject, and the second, with the criticism by the adviser and the comment by Confucius, is an attempt to counter that domination.

42. Wang Xianqian et al., *Junshi*, 1.20–22. The translation is modified from Knoblock, *Xunzi*, 1: 142.

43. This is the result of a different conception of human nature with which Xunzi is operating: a person starts off being "incomplete" (*buquan* 不全) and "impure" (*bucui* 不粹), and only after much effort does he become *chengren* 成人, or John Knoblock's "the perfected man"; his effort is directed at fulfilling these inherent deficiencies, not overcoming them.

Chapter 4

1. I also mentioned *anxing* 闇行 ("acting in the dark") in chapter 3.

2. He Ning, *Huainanzi jishi*, 447–62. The translation is modified from Major et al., *Huainanzi*, 218, especially n28. For the parallel to this passage in the text from the *Wenzi* called "Pure Sincerity" (Jingcheng 精誠), see Wang Liqi, *Wenzi shuyi*, 66–71.

3. He Ning, *Huainanzi jishi*, 722. The translation is modified from Major et al., *Huainanzi*, 361. A later statement from the same text is likely also related: 釋近期遠, 塞矣 "To abandon what is close at hand in expectation of what is far-off is to obstruct one's path." The character *qi* 期 is emended from 斯 following a proposal by Wang Niansun.

4. The character *zhi* 之 added, following Wang Niansun.

5. Li Xiangfeng, *Guanzi jiaozhu*, 25–31. The translations for this and the commentary cited later are modified from W. Allyn Rickett, *Guanzi: Political, Eco-*

nomic, and Philosophical Essays from Early China (Princeton: Princeton University Press, 1985–1998), 1: 71–72.

6. Li Xiangfeng, *Guanzi jiaozhu*, 1170–75.

7. Li Xiangfeng, *Guanzi jiaozhu*, 45–47, and the accompanying commentary in Li Xiangfeng, *Guanzi jiaozhu*, 1186–90. The translations of the two passages are modified from Rickett, *Guanzi*, 87.

8. Takigawa Kametarō and Mizusawa Toshitada, *Shiji huizhu kaozheng fu jiaobu*, 4.12–13. The translation is modified from Nienhauser Jr., ed., *The Grand Scribe's Records*, 1: 58.

9. Zuo Songchao, *Shuoyuan jizheng*, 21–23. Another account can be found in Mao's 毛 commentary to "Long Drawn-out" (Mian 縣) in the *Book of Odes*; see Li Xueqin, ed., *Maoshi zhengyi*, 1165.

10. A parallel to this passage can be found in a text from the *School Sayings of Confucius* (Kongzi jiayu 孔子家語) called "Fondness for Life" (Hao sheng 好生), though without the reference to "not acting" (*wu wei*); see Yang Zhaoming 楊朝明, *Kongzi jiayu tongjie—fu chutu ziliao yu xiangguan yanjiu* 孔子家語通解——附出土資料相關研究 (Taipei: Wanjuanlou, 2005), 123–24. Perhaps the expression was purposely edited out. As for the expression "not moving" (*budong*) this is, of course, reminiscent of the discussion of the "unstirred mind" (*budong xin* 不動心) in Mencius 2A2; see Jiao Xun, *Mengzi zhengyi*, 187–220. This is consistent with the *Garden of Sayings* in the sense that the equanimity of an unstirred mind is what enables one to accomplish one's goal. A restless mind, by contrast, only has the appearance of being active when in fact it gets little done.

11. Cf. the text from the *Huainanzi* called "Among Others" (Renjian 人間), with the statement: 夫有陰德者必有陽報, 有陰行者必有昭名 "The potency of *yin* will certainly meet the response of *yang*; he who conducts himself nobly in obscurity will certainly have a resplendent name"; see He Ning, *Huainanzi jishi*, 1254–55. The translation is modified from Major et al., *Huainanzi*, 727. Parallels can be found in the text from the *Wenzi* called "Supreme Virtue" (Shangde), in Wang Liqi, *Wenzi shuyi*, 302–3; and the text in the *Garden of Sayings* called "Valuing Virtue" (Gui de 貴德), in Zuo Songchao, *Shuoyuan jizheng*, 246–49.

12. Cf. the *Laozi* 老子, chap. 46, for which the received text has the following: 天下有道, 却走馬以糞; 天下無道, 戎馬生於郊 "When the Way prevails in the empire, fleet-footed horses are relegated to moving manure; when the Way does not prevail in the empire, war-horses breed on the border"; see Shima Kunio, *Rōshi kōsei*. The translation is modified from Lau, *Tao Te Ching*.

13. *Zuo chi* and *lu chen* can also be found in the *Zhuangzi*, in "In the World of Men" (Renjianshi) and "Ze Yang," respectively. We can interpret those usages in a way that is consistent with how they appear in the passage from the *Huainanzi*. See Wang Shumin, *Zhuangzi jiaoquan*, 117–36, 1015–18.

14. We may compare this discussion to Heshanggong's commentary on the *Laozi* chap. 25. Under the original phrase *Tian fa Dao* 天法道 ("Heaven takes the

Way for its model"), Heshanggong offers the following elaboration: 道清靜不言, 陰行精氣, 萬物自成也 "The Way is tranquil, quiescent, and does not speak, and it secretly circulates the essential energy, so the myriad things are spontaneously perfected"; see Shima Kunio, *Rōshi kōsei*. The translation is modified from Erkes, *Ho-Shang-Kung's Commentary on Lao-Tse*.

15. Jiang Lihong, *Shangjun shu zhuizhi*, 110–13.

16. Shima Kunio, *Rōshi kōsei*. The translation is from Lau, *Tao Te Ching*.

17. Wang Xianqian et al., *Junshi*, 15.14. The translation is modified from Knoblock, *Xunzi*, 3: 105.

18. Wu Zeyu 吳則虞, *Yanzi chunqiu jishi* 晏子春秋集釋 (Beijing: Guojia tushuguan, 2011), *juan* 5, 252–58. For parallels to this passage, see Shi Guangying 石光瑛, *Xinxu jiaoshi* 新序校釋 (Beijing: Zhonghua, 2001), 112–20; and Xu Weiyu 許維遹, *Hanshi waizhuan jishi* 韓詩外傳集釋 (Beijing: Zhonghua, 1980), *juan* 8, 289–90. James Robert Hightower's translation of the latter provides the basis for my translation of the passage from the *Spring and Autumn Annals of Master Yan*; see *Han shih wai chuan: Han Ying's Illustrations of the Didactic Application of the Classic of Songs* (Cambridge, MA: Harvard University Press, 1952), 272–73. For an alternative translation, see Olivia Milburn, *The Spring and Autumn Annals of Master Yan* (Leiden: Brill, 2016), 322–23. Note that the Yanzi story is also mentioned in a text from the *Discourses on Salt and Iron* (Yantie lun 鹽鐵論) called "Extolling the Rites" (Chong li 崇禮); see Wang Liqi 王利器, *Yantie lun jiaozhu* 鹽鐵論校注 (Beijing: Zhonghua, 1992), 437–44.

19. The remark by Shi Guangying is actually found in the same author's commentary to the *Sources Newly Arranged* (Xinxu 新序), cited in the previous note.

20. Wang Xianqian et al., *Junshi*, 15.22–25. The translation is modified from Knoblock, *Xunzi*, 3:109–10.

21. Cf. the series of anecdotes about an archer who mistakes a stone for a tiger and shoots it, penetrating it with his arrow. In the transmitted literary record, this archer is variously identified as Xiong Quzi 熊渠子, Yang Youji 養由基, and Li Guang 李廣. In two versions of the story found in the *Sources Newly Arranged* and *Outer Commentaries of the Han Tradition of the Odes* (Hanshi waizhuan 韓詩外傳), the account reports that the incident takes place at night, when the archer is *yexing* ("walking by night"). While some of the discussions praise the archer for his *cheng* ("sincerity"), others emphasize the theme of nonaction: the archer is able to penetrate the stone precisely because he had no intention to do so, just as the ruler is at his best when he does not act purposefully. See Shi Guangying, *Xinxu jiaoshi*, 615–21; Xu Weiyu, *Hanshi waizhuan jishi*, *juan* 6, 230–31; Takigawa Kametarō and Mizusawa Toshitada, *Shiji huizhu kaozheng fu jiaobu*, 109.9–10; Wang Xianqian, *Hanshu buzhu*, 3941; and Chen Qiyou, *Lüshi chunqiu xin jiaoshi*, 514. Just who exactly is the real protagonist of the story is the subject of Wang Chong's 王充 (27–ca. 100) discussion in an essay in the *Disquisitions* (Lunheng 論衡) called

"Exaggerations of the Literati" (Ruzeng 儒增); see Huang Hui 黃暉, *Lunheng jiaoshi* 論衡校釋 (Beijing: Zhonghua, 1990), 362–65.

22. Other references to the same parable can be found in a text from the *Zhuangzi* called "The Old Fisherman" (Yufu 漁父), in Wang Shumin, *Zhuangzi jiaoquan*, 1229–49; a text in the *Garden of Sayings* called "Upright Remonstrations" (Zhengjian 正諫), in Zuo Songchao, *Shuoyuan jizheng*, 601–9; and a text in the *Huainanzi* called "Boundless Discourses" (Fanlun 氾論), in He Ning, *Huainanzi jishi*, 980–81. None of these is exactly like "Dispelling Blindness," but they are similar enough to warrant a few comments. To begin with the closer *Huainanzi* passage, the discussion there betrays the same concern with the real versus the unreal that also underlies Xunzi's essay. The same is true with "The Old Fisherman," which repeatedly emphasizes the notion of "authenticity" (*zhen* 真). Another theme addressed by this text is that of nonaction, and this is what one finds in "Correct Remonstrations" as well.

23. Wang Xianqian et al., *Junshi*, 15.12. The translation is modified from Knoblock, *Xunzi*, 3: 104.

24. For another correspondence between the different parts of "Dispelling Blindness," we might refer to another of Xunzi's illustrations of mental confusion: 水動而景搖, 人不以定美惡, 水埶玄也 "When water is moving and reflections waver, men do not use it to determine their beauty or ugliness. The circumstances of the water make for deception." This corresponds to the earlier statement: 故人心譬如槃水, 正錯而勿動, 則湛濁在下而清明在上, 則足以見鬚眉而察膚理矣 "Hence the human mind may be compared to a pan of water. If you place the pan upright and do not stir the water up, the mud will sink to the bottom, and the water on top will be clear and pure enough to see your beard and eyebrows and to examine the lines of your skin"; see Wang Xianqian et al., *Junshi*, 15.18;. The translation is modified from Knoblock, *Xunzi*, 3: 107. Following Hao Yixing 郝懿行 (1757–1825), I restore the character *fu* 膚 in the second statement.

25. This translation reflects Yang Liang's 楊倞 (ninth century) understanding of the text.

26. Wang Xianqian et al., *Junshi*, 15.1–20; and the corresponding translations modified from Knoblock, *Xunzi*, 3: 100–107.

27. See my article for some additional examples: "'Fan wu liu xing' kaoshi sanze."

28. See *The Lost Texts of Confucius's Grandson*, chap. 1. This other passage from "Dispelling Blindness" concerns a man who resides in a stone cave, named Ji 伋, and it appears immediately before the parable about Juan Shuliang. A quick comparison of the two shows that they are connected in more than one way. Ji is someone who lives alone, whereas Juan Shuliang's name, as I point out presently, reflects a situation where aloneness is also an important theme. The juxtaposition of these two figures in "Dispelling Blindness" is not an accident. Perhaps the relation between them is similar to that between the newly excavated

"Five Conducts" (Wuxing) and its commentary. The former allots a central place to the topic of aloneness (which I believe also underlies Xunzi's discussion of Ji), and the latter, in discussing the mind, introduces the finer distinction between the inner and outer mind (a reason for Xunzi's attack on Juan Shuliang, in my view).

29. He Ning, *Huainanzi jishi*, 229–30. The translation is modified from Major et al., *Huainanzi*, 367. For the usage of *dun* 遁, cf. the text from the *Annals of Lü Buwei* called "Making Life the Foundation" (Ben sheng), which contains the statement: 世之貴富者, 其於聲色滋味也多惑之, 日夜求, 幸而得之則遁焉 "The great majority of honored and wealthy people today are deluded in regard to sounds, colors, and rich flavors. They seek these things every day and every night. If by good fortune they obtain them, they abandon themselves to them"; see Chen Qiyou, *Lüshi chunqiu xin jiaoshi*, 21–22; and the translation from Knoblock and Riegel, *The Annals of Lü Buwei*, 65. The commentator Gao You glosses *dun* 遁 as the following: 流逸不能自禁也 "dissolute and being unable to restrain oneself," and Chen Qiyou explains that this is reading it as *xun* 循, also written 巡. These meanings are related in that self-abandonment or self-deception means that one has veered away from the right path, having "escaped" or "run astray."

30. Li Xueqin, ed., *Maoshi zhengyi*, 868. The line is also quoted in the *Analects* 8.3; here I follow the translation from Lau, *The Analects*.

31. One possible explanation for this is that *Yuan* "abyss" is the name of this figure, and *Duliang* "single log" his cognomen. Such understanding of the semantic relation between the name and the cognomen corresponds to the conventions of ancient naming practices such as explicated in Wang Yinzhi 王引之, "Chunqiu mingzi jiegu" 春秋名字解詁, in *Jingyi shuwen* 經義述聞 (Shanghai: Shanghai guji, 2016), *juan* 22–23. As for the dates of this figure, see the discussion of Huan Yuan in Qian Mu's 錢穆 *Xian Qin zhuzi xinian* 先秦諸子繫年 (Taipei: Lianjing, 1994), 238–43, which gives 360–280 BCE. For a recent study that also brings together many of the sources on Huan Yuan, see Rao Zongyi 饒宗頤, "Juanzi 'Qinxin' kao—you Guodian yaqin tan Laozi menren de qinxue" 涓子《琴心》考——由郭店雅琴探老子門人的琴學, in *Rao Zongyi ershi shijie xueshu wenji* 饒宗頤二十世紀學術文集 (Taipei: Xin wenfeng, 2003), 4: 535–50.

32. The former is "Memoir of Mengzi and Xun Qing" (Mengzi Xun Qing liezhuan 孟子荀卿列傳); see Takigawa Kametarō and Mizusawa Toshitada, *Shiji huizhu kaozheng fu jiaobu*, 74.12. For the latter, see Gu Shi 顧實, *Hanshu yiwen zhi jiangshu* 漢書藝文志講疏 (Shanghai: Shanghai guji, 1987), 118.

33. Cf. the text in the *Huainanzi* called "Originating in the Way" (Yuandao), which describes how Shun 舜 in his days as a fisherman exerted such positive influence on his companions that they yielded to one another the best fishing spots: 釣於河濱, 朞年而漁者爭處湍瀨, 以曲隈深潭相予 "He fished on the riverbank. After a year the fishermen fought to occupy the rapids and shallows while they gave the remote coves and deep pools to one another"; see He Ning, *Huainanzi jishi*, 46–48; and the translation from Major et al., *Huainanzi*, 59. *Yuan* as "origin" corresponds to the "remote coves," and as "abyss" the "deep pools." Incidentally, the same passage

goes on to talk about *xinxing* "the movement of the mind," an expression closely related to *yexing*, as pointed out earlier in this chapter.

34. These include the text from the *Huainanzi* called "Originating in the Way" (Yuandao), where the man's name appears as Juan Xuan 娟嬛; see He Ning, *Huainanzi jishi*, 26. Another notable example is Li Shan's 李善 (d. 689 CE) commentary to "Seven Stimuli" (Qifa 七發) by Mei Sheng 枚乘 (ca. 210–138); see *Wenxuan* 文選 (Shanghai: Shanghai guji, 1986), 1572–73. Here, Huan Yuan's name appears as Yuan Xuan 蜎蠉. Note that the ancient lexicographical work *Approaching Refinement* (Erya 爾雅) glosses *yuan* 蜎 as *xuan* 蠉; see Hao Yixing 郝懿行, *Erya yishu* 爾雅義疏 (Jinan: Qi Lu, 2010), 3663–64. Qian Mu speculates on this basis that *yuanxuan* 蜎蠉 means "bait," another word related to fishing; see Qian Mu, *Xian Qin zhuzi xinian*, 240. Note, additionally, that Li Shan cites from a lost *Song Yu ji* 宋玉集, which reports that Song Yu and a fellow student received fishing instructions at a location called *xuanyuan* 玄淵 ("dark abyss"). This information now appears in the prefatory statement to "Exposition Poem on Fishing" (Diao fu 釣賦), attributed to the legendary Warring States poet Song Yu; see *Taiping yulan* 太平御覽 (woodblock ed., ca. 1022–1063; Beijing: Zhonghua, 1960), 834.6. For this last item, Qian Mu suggests that it is an instance where the name of Huan Yuan has been corrupted into a place name: 凡此皆俗談小說之引而益遠者 "All of this is due to vulgar talks and petty discussions, which cite the information and cause it to be increasing removed from the truth." This is a matter that I take up below, for I think the reverse of this explanation is also possible, that it was the place name that gave rise to the personal name.

35. For a similar instance where the name of a figure becomes tied with the stories about him, one can turn to the text in the *Zhuangzi* called "Mastering Life" (Da sheng), where Yan Yuan 顏淵, the famous disciple of Confucius, reports that he once crossed the *Shangshen zhi yuan* 觴深之淵 ("gulf at Goblet Deeps") where he encountered a ferryman who "handled the boat with supernatural skill" (*cao zhou ru shen* 操舟若神); see Wang Shumin, *Zhuangzi jiaoquan*, 681–85; and the translation in Watson, *The Complete Works of Chuang Tzu*, 200–201. Another example is the legendary ancient ruler Shun 舜 (*hjuns): *yun* 允 (*jun?) is both the phonetic with which his name is written in paleographic sources and part of an instruction to which he has been given in the *Analects* 20.1: 允執其中 "To hold truly what is internal to him"; see Cheng Shude, *Lunyu jishi*, 1065–68. The translation is modified from Lau, *Analects*.

36. In suggesting that there is a parallel between Guan Yin and Huan Yuan, I am aware of the argument by Qian Mu that they were actually the same person, though I find it difficult to assess this claim because the former figure is even more obscure than the latter. For this and other references about Guan Yin, see Qian Mu, *Xian Qin zhuzi xinian*, 239–42.

37. Li Xueqin, ed., *Maoshi zhengyi*, 458–60; and the translation from Karlgren, *The Book of Odes*, 113–14.

38. It is for this reason that I did not accept previous proposals to translate Nüju's name as "Woman Crookback" or "Woman Hunchback."

Chapter 5

1. Shima Kunio, *Rōshi kōsei*. The translation is modified from Lau, *Tao Te Ching*.

2. For my reading of the phrase: 載營魄抱一 "When you envelop your bodily soul and embrace Oneness," I follow Yang Xiufang 楊秀芳 in taking *zai* 載 as an exclamation particle that has accidentally crept into text, perhaps from the previous chapter 9. Presumably, this mistake was already in place by the time of the Mawangdui manuscript, our earliest attestation of chapter 10, and it is also reflected in a close parallel to the same text in "Far-off Journey" of *The Songs of the South*. My understanding of *ying* 營 is also based on Yang. For both points, see her article "Lun 'ying po bao yi'" 論「營魄抱一」, in Shi Feng 石鋒 and Peng Gang 彭剛, eds., *Dajiang dongqu: Wang Shiyuan jiaoshou bashisui heshou wenji* 大江東去: 王士元教授八十歲賀壽文集 (Hong Kong: City University of Hong Kong Press, 2013), 353–69.

3. Qiu Xigui, ed., *Changsha Mawangdui Hanmu jianbo jicheng*, 1: 136–37; and the transcription in 6: 172–73. The translation is based on Yates, *Five Lost Classics*, 152–53.

4. For this sentence, note that *cun* 存 ("to exist") corresponds to *cang* 藏 ("to store") and *xie* 挾 ("to clasp") later on. It is also not far from the meanings of *bao* 紆 (保) and *tun* 屯 as "to protect" and "to accumulate," respectively. The sense is that in embracing the principle of Oneness, one should treat it as if it did not exist. Grammatically, it is possible to compare this statement with the *Analects* 15.32: 君子謀道不謀食；耕也，餒在其中矣；學也，祿在其中矣；君子憂道不憂貧 "The gentleman devotes his mind to attaining the Way and not to securing food. Go and till the land and you will end up by being hungry, as a matter of course; study, and you will end up with the salary of an official, as a matter of course"; see Cheng Shude, *Lunyu jishi*, 1119–20; and the translation from Lau, *The Analects*. The juxtaposition of the two verbs *geng* 耕 ("to till the land") and *xue* 學 ("study") corresponds to that of *bao* and *tun* in "Sixteen Canons." If one were to rewrite the statement from this Mawangdui manuscript by modeling it on the *Analects*, one could posit the following: *保也，其如莫存；屯也，其如莫存.

5. Cf. the discussion of the term *zi de* 自得 ("finding it within oneself") from "Far-off Journey" in chapter 1.

6. Emended from the character 慕, following Yu Yue.

7. Li Xiangfeng, *Guanzi jiaozhu*, 780–81. The translations are modified from Rickett, *Guanzi*, 2: 60–61.

8. For the "Inner Workings," see Li Xiangfeng, *Guanzi jiaozhu*, 942–44. The translations are modified from Rickett, *Guanzi*, 2: 49–51.

9. Emended from the character 摶, following Wang Niansun (67–68).

10. Emended from the character 摶, following Wang Niansun (67–68).

11. The characters *xiong* 凶 and *ji* 吉 reversed, following Wang Niansun.

12. The character *de* 得 restored, based on the parallel with "Art of the Mind, Part Two."

13. Cf. another statement from "Inner Workings": 人能正靜, 皮膚裕寬, 耳目聰明, 筋信而骨強 "When man is capable of good judgment and remaining quiescent, his flesh will be plump and full, his ears and eyes sharp and clear, his muscle taut, and his bones sturdy." Both of these can be compared with the discussion in "Great Learning," as we saw in chapter 2, about "virtue making a person shining," such that "when one's mind is broad and his heart generous, his body becomes big and is at ease."

14. Wang Shumin, *Zhuangzi jiaoquan*, 855–84. The translation is modified from Watson, *The Complete Works of Chuang Tzu*, 248–54.

15. This follows Cui Zhuan 崔譔 (third–fourth century), who suggests that *pi* 辟 means *xiang zhuo* 相著 ("to be attached to each other"). As pointed out by several scholars, this is perhaps reading *pi* as *bi* 襞 or *bi* 擘.

16. This discussion also corresponds to a later part of the narrative, where Laozi suggests the following: 夫外韄者不可繁而捉, 將內揵; 內韄者不可繆而捉, 將外揵; 外內韄者, 道德不能持, 而況放道而行者乎 "When outside things trip you up and you can't snare and seize them because they are so numerous, then bar the inside gate. When inside things trip you up and you can't bind and seize them because they are so entangled, then bar the outside gate. If both outside and inside things trip you up, then even the Way and its virtue themselves can't keep you going—much less one who is a mere follower of the Way in his actions." The technical terms *jian* 揵 and *hu* 韄 may be references to more detailed discussions that are only alluded to here, much like the discussion about the eyes, ears, and mind being part of the body may point to the conception of the "heart of hearts." *Jian* is literally a vertical beam used to secure a closed door; one end is set in the ground, while the other is placed at an angle to the horizontal door latch. As for *hu*, it is literally "ties" or "restraints." Cf. the discussion of this passage in Yang Xiufang, "Lun dongci 'jian' de yuyi fazhan" 論動詞「揵」的語義發展, *Zhongguo yuyanxue jikan* 中國語言學集刊 1.2 (2007): 99–115, especially 102–6.

17. We may contrast this with the discussion frequently encountered in the *Zhuangzi* and other Daoist texts that one could become a companion of Heaven, the Way, or the creator of things—a state of being that is more preferable for obvious reasons.

18. Wang Liqi, *Wenzi shuyi*, 104–9. A parallel of this passage can be found in the text from the *Huainanzi* called "Cultivating Effort" (Xiuwu 脩務); see He Ning, *Huainanzi jishi*, 1347–55.

19. Yan Zhenyi 閻振益 and Zhong Xia 鍾夏, *Xinshu jiaozhu* 新書校注 (Beijing: Zhonghua, 2000), 296–301.

20. The characters *ji* 吉 and *xiong* 凶 reversed, following Wang Niansun.

21. It would be difficult to speculate on what these so-called basic rules of self-preservation were based on the account in "Gengsang Chu" alone, given its bias. I would begin with the teachings often ascribed to Yang Zhu, some of which we saw in chapter 3, but they must go back even farther.

22. Of course, Nanrong Chu's request also corresponds to Gengsang Chu's advice, given earlier in the same text, about "clinging fast to life" (*bao rusheng*).

23. As noted by several commentators, this last point from Laozi's remarks and the language used to make it bear a close resemblance to chapter 55 of the *Laozi*.

24. Both can be linked with a third expression "mysterious sameness" (*xuantong* 玄同) in chapter 56 of the *Laozi*; see Shima Kunio, *Rōshi kōsei*.

25. Yan Zhenyi and Zhong Xia, *Xinshu jiaozhu*, 304.

26. Shima Kunio, *Rōshi kōsei*. The translation is from Lau, *Tao Te Ching*. Cf. also Erkes, *Ho-Shang-Kung's Commentary on Lao-Tse*.

27. Chen Qiyou, *Han Feizi xin jiaozhu*, 421–22. The translation is modified from W. K. Liao, *The Complete Works of Han Fei Tzŭ*, 199–200.

28. As noted by previous scholars, another indication of the integrity of "All Things Flow into Form" is that the first part asks what enables plants to grow and what enables beasts to cry (slips 12a + 13b), whereas the second part replies that these phenomena are due, once again, to the principle of "Oneness" (slips 21, 13a).

29. In Qian Mu, *Zhongguo xueshu xixiang shi luncong (er)* 中國學術思想史論叢 (二) (Taipei: Lianjing, 1994), 18: 25–74.

30. In the same way, I would disagree with Qian Mu on the placement of Mencius. Rather than seeing him as clinging onto the earlier, more primordial view of the cosmos, I would suggest that such a view was never completely rejected in Confucian thought, and that it remained visible in the Guodian manuscripts, which draw a distinction between "the Heavenly" (*tian* 天) and "the human" (*ren* 人) and leave little question that their priority lies with the former. In contrast to this, Mencius makes a conscious decision to step away from the Heavenly and focus instead on the human.

Concluding Remarks

1. The classic study on this topic is Hu Houxuan 胡厚宣, "Chong lun 'yu yiren' wenti" 重論「余一人」問題, *Guwenzi yanjiu* 古文字研究 6 (1981): 15–33.

2. Some of the studies that I have found useful in considering the issues raised here are Hellmut Wilhelm, "Bemerkungen zur T'ien-wen Frage," *Monumenta Serica* 10 (1945): 427–32; Paul Demiéville, "Enigmes taoistes," in *Silver Jubilee Volume of the Zinbun-Kagaku Kenkyushyo, Kyoto University* (Kyoto: Kyoto University, 1954), 54–60; and Rao Zongyi 饒宗頤, "'Tianwen' wenti de yuanliu—fawen wenxue zhi tantao"《天問》文體的源流——發問文學之探討, in *Rao Zongyi ershi shiji xueshu wenji* 饒宗頤二十世紀學術文集 (Taipei: Xin wenfeng, 2003), 11: 35–56.

3. Wang Shumin, *Zhuangzi jiaoquan*, 505–9. The translation is from Watson, *The Complete Works of Chuang Tzu*, 154–55.

4. Reading *zhen* 緘 as *xian* 咸, glossed *yin* 引, following a variant cited by Lu Deming.

5. This refers to the legendary revelation of the *Luoshu* 洛書, a text written on the back of a turtle emerging from the Luo River.

6. The characters *chong* 重 and *se* 塞 reduplicated, following Chen Qiyou.

7. Emended from the character 伐, following Wang Niansun.

8. Emended from the character 實, following Chen Qiyou.

9. Emended from the character 北, following Wang Niansun.

10. Emended from the character 怪, following Sun Yirang 孫詒讓 (1848–1908).

11. Chen Qiyou, *Lüshi chunqiu xin jiaoshi*, 1103–4. The translation is modified from Knoblock and Riegel, *The Annals of Lü Buwei*, 425.

12. Qiu Xigui, ed., *Changsha Mawangdui Hanmu jianbo jicheng*, 2: 203–11, and the transcription in 6: 139–51. The translation is based on Harper, *Early Chinese Medical Literature*, 393.

13. The same figure also appears as Wu Cheng Zhao 務成昭 in the text in the *Xunzi* called "The Great Compendium" (Dalue 大略); see Wang Xianqian et al., *Junshi*, 19.5–6. There is also a work associated with the same figure, titled *The Secret Way of Wu Chengzi* (Wu Chengzi yindao 務成子陰道), recorded in the bibliographical treatise of the *History of the Former Han*; see Gu Shi, *Hanshu yiwen zhi jiangshu*, 242.

14. For details, see *The Lost Texts of Confucius's Grandson*, chap. 5.

15. Li Xiangfeng, *Guanzi jiaozhu*, 937–42. The translation is from Rickett, *Guanzi*, 2: 42–49.

16. Of course, one of the neighboring texts of "Grand One Gives Birth to Water," "Five Conducts," does speak of the mind, but only in a rudimentary sense because it does not attribute any inherent capacity to the mind.

17. For "Doctrine of the Mean," see Li Xueqin, ed., *Liji zhengyi*, 1661–712.

18. Shima Kunio, *Rōshi kōsei*; and Wang Shumin, *Zhuangzi jiaoquan*, 288–303.

19. Here one might raise the objection that if "Grand One Gives Birth to Water" was indeed earlier than "All Things Flow into Form," then why would the latter text still raise all those questions when the answer was readily available in the former? But an objection such as this could only be sustained if one actually took the questions literally. In fact, as previously discussed, the questions of "All Things Flow into Form" are rhetorical in nature.

20. The characters *shu* 殊 and *neng* 能 restored, following Wang Xianqian.

21. Little is known about the two figures. For some scattered references to the said teachings, particularly *huo shi*, see Ikeda Tomohisa's 池田知久 discussion of the term *ziran* 自然 ("spontaneity") in *Daojia sixiang de xin yanjiu—yi Zhuangzi wei zhongxin* 道家思想的新研究——以《莊子》為中心 (Zhengzhou: Zhongzhou guji, 2009), 536–47. Cf. also D. C. Lau's discussion of the *Mengzi* 1A6 in *Mencius*, xxxiv–xxxv.

22. The character *ce* 測 restored, following Wang Shumin.

23. Wang Shumin, *Zhuangzi jiaoquan*, 1031–42. The translation is modified from Watson, *The Complete Works of Chuang Tzu*, 289–93.

24. Cf. the statement from "All Things Flow into Form" (slips 21, 13A, 12B, 22): 肱 (一) 生兩, 兩生弎 (三), 弎 (三) 生女〈四〉, 女〈四〉城 (成) 結 "One begets two, two begets three, three begets four, and four are crisscrossed." The resemblance to chapter 42 of the *Laozi* is obvious: 道生一, 一生二, 二生三, 三生萬物 "The Way begets one; one begets two; two begets three; three begets the myriad creatures"; see Shima Kunio, *Rōshi kōsei*, and the translation from Lau, *Tao Te Ching*. For further discussion on the debate between the Way and One, see *The Lost Texts of Confucius's Grandson*, chap. 4.

Index

acting in the dark, 55–56. *See also* night, journey in
Ai shiming 哀時命. *See* "Alas That My Lot Was Not Cast,"
"Alas That My Lot Was Not Cast," 23–24
"All Things Flow into Form," vii, 95–97
  bifurcated structure of, 101
  Chinese transcription of, 9–11
  English translation of, 3–7
  ethical question discussed in, 31–42
  "Grand One Gives Birth to Water" as preceding, 101–2
  heart of hearts formulation, 43–61
  implication of journey in night, 63–77
  mind as portrayed in, 31–42
  notion of nonaction in, 66–69
  numinousness of ghosts, 90–93
  and Oneness, 87–89
  publication of, vii–viii
  reading "Dispelling Blindness" against, 69–73, 79–93
  sincerity, 31–42
  sources of, 97–103
  and *Zhuangzi*, viii–xi, 15–29
Analects 12.1, 44–46
arriving at dawn, phrase, 18, 25, 32, 95

"Art of the Mind, Part Two," *Guanzi*, 81–83

bai 白 ("to reveal"), 32–33
"Basic Annals of Zhou," *Grand Scribe's Records*, 64–65
Ben sheng 本生. *See* "Making Life the Foundation"
Book of Odes, 23–24, 75, 119
Bu Liangyi 卜梁倚, 16

Celestial Emperor, 20
"Charting the Policies," *Book of Lord Shang*, 56–57, 67
chongshang 重傷. *See* double injury
Chuci 楚辭. *See Songs of the South, The*
"Commentaries on Laozi's Teachings," *Han Feizi*, 89–90
Confucius, 45–46, 55–56
"Cosmologies of the Commentaries of the *Book of Changes* and the *Records of the Rites*," 92

Da zongshi" 大宗師. *See* "Great and Venerable Teacher, The"
Daoshu 道術. *See* "Methods of the Way"
Daren fu 大人賦. *See* "Exposition Poem on the Mighty One"

141

Daxue 大學. *See* "Great Learning"
Di 帝. *See* Celestial Emperor
Didu 杜杜. *See* "Solitary Pyrus Tree"
"Dispelling Blindness," 63, 67, 69–73, 87
  reading "All Things Flow into Form" against, 79–93
double injury, 49–52
du 獨 ("alone"), 17–18, 23–24, 59
Duke Zhao of Lu 魯昭公, 45

Erbing 二柄. *See* "Two Handles, The"
"Exhortation to Learning, An," Xunzi, 60–61
"Exhortation to Learning, An," *New Documents*, 85
Explaining Graphs and Analyzing Characters, 24
"Exposition Poem on the Mighty One," 20

"Fan wu liu xing." *See* "All Things Flow into Form"
"Far-off Journey," 17
"Five Conducts," 34–35, 53, 101–2, 132
Fuzi 宓子, 55

Gateway of the Manifold Secrets, The, 35
Gengsang Chu," *Zhuangzi*, 35–36, 79–80, 83–87
"Gentlemen Enact the Rites, The," 43, 45–47, 49, 59, 61
ghosts, numinousness of, 90–93
"Giving Away a Throne," *Zhuangzi*, 49–52
Graham, A. C., 50
"Grand One Gives Birth to Water," 33–34, 93, 101–2
Grand Scribe's Records, 75

"Great and Venerable Teacher, The," *Zhuangzi*
  comparisons, 17–29
  novice-mentor dialogue, 15–17
"Great Learning," 36–37

Han Feizi, 41
Hanshu 漢書. *See History of the Former Han*
Hawkes, David, 18
heart of hearts, formulation of, 53–55
  conceptions of self-struggle, 43–49
  double injury, 50–52
  indebtedness, 53–54
  physical well-being, 50–53
  sincerity, 55–56
  text comparisons, 44–46
  theme of freedom, 49–50
  Xunzi essay, 60–61
  zhong 中 versus *chong* 沖, 60–61
  zi sheng 自勝 expressions, 56–59
History of the Former Han, 75
Hua ce 畫策. *See* "Charting the Policies"
Huainanzi, vii, 21

If the mind does not prevail over the mind, expression, 5, 31–32, 43, 53, 56, 73
"Illustrations of Laozi's Teachings," Han Feizi, 46–49
inaction (*wuwei* 無為), 18. *See also* nonaction
"Inner Workings," *Guanzi*, 82–83, 102

Jade Maiden, 20
jian du 見獨 ("seeing one's aloneness"), 17
Jie bi 解蔽. *See* "Dispelling Blindness"
Jie Lao 解老. *See* "Commentaries on Laozi's Teachings"

Jingcheng 精誠. *See* "Pure Sincerity"
Jingshen 精神. *See* "Quintessential Spirit"
Jiutan 九嘆. *See* "Nine Laments"
Juan Shuliang 涓蜀梁, 77
Jubei 具備. *See* "On Necessary Conditions and Preparations"
Jundao 君道. *See* "Lord's Way, The,"
Junzi wei li 君子為禮. *See* "Gentlemen Enact the Rites, The"

King Ling of Chu 楚靈王, 45
"Knowing the Measure," *Annals of Lü Buwei*, 98–99

Lan ming 覽冥. *See* "Surveying Obscurities"
Laozi, 21–22
Li sao 離騷. *See* "On Encountering Trouble"
Liu An 劉安, 21
Liu Xiang 劉向, 17
"Lord's Way, The," *Garden of Sayings*, 65
Lunyu 論語. See *Analects*

"Making Life the Foundation," *Annals of Lü Buwei*, 50–53
Mengzi, 27–29, 35
"Methods of the Way," *New Documents*, 88–89
Miucheng 繆稱. *See* "Profound Precepts"
moral self-cultivation, 34–35
movement of the mind, 64

Nanbo Zikui 南伯子葵, 15–17
Neiye 內業. *See* "Inner Workings"
night, journey in. *See also* acting in the dark
 defining parameters of, 63–64
 nonaction, 64–69

Oneness, 72–75
 ruler's attraction to subjects, 63–65
 single log, 75–77
"Nine Laments," 17
nonaction, 64–69, 80–81, 95. *See also* inaction
Nüyu 女偊, 15–17

"On Assumers," *Han Feizi*, 40
"On Encountering Trouble," 19–20
"On Necessary Conditions and Preparations," *Annals of Lü Buwei*, 55–56
Oneness, 72–75
 embracing, 79–82
 grasping, 82
"Outpouring of Sad Thoughts, The," "Nine Declarations," 22–23

pai 排 ("to push open"), 20
paring down what is completed, expression, 5, 31–33, 95, 101
Peng Xian 彭咸, 17
"Profound Precepts," *Huainanzi*, 64, 75–77
"Pure Sincerity," *Wenzi*, 85

Qian Mu 錢穆, 92
qiongqiong 煢煢 (also written 惸惸), 17
Quanxue 勸學. *See* "Exhortation to Learning, An"
"Quintessential Spirit," *Huainanzi*, 48–50

Rang wang 讓王. *See* "Giving Away a Throne"
Ren bai wei cha 人白為察. *See* revealing oneself for inspection by others
"Responses of the Way," *Huainanzi*, 56
revealing oneself for inspection by others, expression, 32, 35–37, 40

Rong Cheng 容成, 100

"Saddened by Sufferings," "Nine Laments," 17
self-satisfaction, 19, 33
Shang Yang 商鞅, 56
Shanghai Museum, 22
Shiji 史記. See *Grand Scribe's Records*
Shijing 詩經. See *Book of Odes*
Shiliujing 十六經. See "Sixteen Canons"
Shiwen 十問. See "Ten Questions"
Shuo yi 說疑. See "On Assumers"
Shuowen jiezi 說文解字. See *Explaining Graphs and Analyzing Characters*
Si meiren 思美人. See "Thinking of a Fair One"
Sima Xiangru 司馬相如, 20
sincerity, 55–56
"Sixteen Canons," 80–81
"Solitary Pyrus Tree," 77
Songs of the South, The, 17, 22, 32
Spring and Autumn Annals of Master Yan, 67–69
"Surveying Obscurities," *Huaninanzi*, 63–67

Taiyi sheng shui 太一生水. See "Grand One Gives Birth to Water"
Tianyun 天運. See "Turning of Heaven, The"
"Ten Questions," 27–29, 99–101
"Thinking of a Fair One," "Nine Declarations," 17
"Turning of Heaven, The," *Zhuangzi*, 97–98
"Two Handles, The," *Han Feizi*, 39–40

Wang Yi 王逸, 17
wang 望 ("to look from afar"), 20
Warring States period, xii, 23–25, 33, 37, 41, 50, 75, 92

"Way of the Sovereign, The," *Han Feizi*, 38–39
weiyi 逶迤, 25–26
well-being, concern with, 49–52
"Wielding the Scepter," *Han Feizi*, 37–38
Wuma Qi, 55
wuwei 無為, 18. See inaction
Wuxing 五行. See "Five Conducts"

Xiao cheng 削成. See paring down what is completed
Xin bu sheng xin 心不勝心. See If the mind does not prevail over the mind
Xinshu xia 心術下. See "Art of the Mind, Part Two"
xinxing 心行. See also movement of the mind
Xunzi, vii, 60–61, 63, 69–73

Yan Zhitui 顏之推, 25
Yang quan 揚權. See "Wielding the Scepter"
Yanzi chunqiu 晏子春秋. See *Spring and Autumn Annals of Master Yan*
yexing 夜行. See acting in the dark; night, journey in
ying ning 攖寧, 16–17, 24–26
Yizhuan yu Xiao Dai liji zhong zhi yuzhou lun 易傳與小戴禮記中之宇宙論. See "Cosmologies of the Commentaries of the *Book of Changes* and the *Records of the Rites*"
Youku 憂苦. See "Saddened by Sufferings"
Yuanyou 遠遊. See "Far-off Journey)
Yu Lao 喻老. See "Illustrations of Laozi's Teachings"
Yunü 玉女. See Jade Maiden

"Ze Yang," *Zhuangzi*, 103–9
zhao che 朝徹. *See* arriving at dawn, phrase
zhengzheng 眐眐, 24
zhongmiao zhi men 眾妙之門, 22. *See also* Gateway of the Manifold Secrets, The (phrase)
Zhi du 知度. *See* "Knowing the Measure"

Zhou benji 周本紀. *See* "Basic Annals of Zhou"
Zhu Xi 朱熹, 35
Zhudao 主道. *See* "Way of the Sovereign, The"
zi de 自得. *See* self-satisfaction
zi ruo 自若, 33
Zichan 子產, 41–42